AWAKENING
The Season that Brought Notre Dame Back

This book is book is available in quantity at special discounts for your group or organization.
For further information, contact:

Triumph Books LLC
814 North Franklin Street
Chicago, Illinois 60610
Phone: (312) 337-0747
www.triumphbooks.com

Printed in U.S.A.
ISBN: 978-1-60078-843-7

South Bend Tribune
Writers: Eric Hansen, Al Lesar, Bob Wieneke
Photographers: James Brosher, Robert Franklin
Copy Editing: Fred Dodd, Agnes Geiger, Todd Merchant
Bill Bilinski, Sports Editor
Santiago Flores, Visuals Editor
Marketing: Elisabeth Clark
Cover Design: Jen Smith
Tim Harmon, Executive Editor
Kim Wilson, President and Publisher

Content packaged by Mojo Media, Inc.
Joe Funk: Editor
Jason Hinman: Creative Director

Front and back cover photos by South Bend Tribune/ROBERT FRANKLIN

In appreciation for Coach Parseghian's contribution to this book, a donation has been made to the Ara Parseghian Medical Research Foundation, which supports efforts to fight Niemann-Pick Type C disease and related neurodegenerative disorders.

This is an unofficial publication. This book is in no way affiliated with, licensed by, or endorsed by the NCAA or the University of Notre Dame.

Several of the news and feature articles in this volume refer to Lennay Kekua, her relationship with All-American linebacker Manti Te'o and her death just before the Michigan State game in September. The world now knows that Kekua's existence was a hoax. This book, however, is a record of the remarkable Notre Dame season as it unfolded. Thus we have chosen to include each article as it originally appeared in the *South Bend Tribune*.

South Bend Tribune/ROBERT FRANKLIN

CONTENTS

Foreword

By Ara Parseghian

I heard it when I was at Northwestern, before I came to Notre Dame. I've heard it many times after I left Notre Dame, that Notre Dame football would never be back. The reality is they were in a down cycle, which all schools go through, but I never believed it was forever.

As I look back, when I came to Notre Dame after the 1963 season, they were in a down cycle. When Lou Holtz came in, they were in a down cycle. And you heard the same reasons and excuses each time—the schedule's too tough, the academics are too difficult. And then someone like Brian Kelly comes along and proves it can be done without changing or compromising any of those standards and principles. I have to say I was kind of irritated when I read early in the year that Notre Dame was supposedly irrelevant. I think this team proved Notre Dame is very relevant.

The plan I had when I came in was multifaceted. There wasn't just one thing to address in the down cycle, when you've been below .500 for the last five years. A big part of the plan had to do with the players — rebuilding their confidence, making them believe they could win. You can't keep getting hit over the head. At some point you start to believe you can't get out of the way. You have to encourage confidence, but there has to be a payoff. That payoff comes when you win your first game. That first game of the season is so important. In my 25 years of coaching, I lost one season opener. So you build off of that. It's tough to build when you get your ass beat in your first game.

What I liked about this team and the way it was built was the chemistry they had. I saw a documentary that was made leading up to the Miami game and it showed the team in the locker room and in practice. I really liked what I saw. There's a guy on the team who's the leader, a guy who's the clown. When you saw that mixture and the camaraderie on the field, I knew this was going to be a tough team to beat. They just had all of those necessary ingredients.

I really like the quarterback, Everett Golson. I think he has terrific potential. He was slow coming along with the system Brian Kelly was espousing, but Kelly stuck with that system, and it paid off. I liked Brian Kelly from the start. He's won everywhere he's been. I thought he'd win at Notre Dame. I just wasn't counting on this kind of season this early. With the schedule they had, I thought they'd go 9-3. But with each passing week, I saw things that gave them a chance to go undefeated.

The question now is will they be able to sustain the success. It's a lot easier to get to the top of the mountain than it is to stay there. You almost become a victim of your own success. Every team they play next year will get a plume in its hat if it knocks off Notre Dame. It's always been that way, but it will intensify now. But I like what Brian Kelly is building. I think they can stay on the top of the hill if they continue to do the things that got them there. If that happens, Notre Dame will be back for a long, long time. ■

Ara Parseghian
January 2013

Ara Parseghian was head coach of the Fighting Irish football team from 1964 to 1974. In those 11 seasons, his teams had a 95-17-4 record and won two national titles, in 1966 and 1973.

Ara Parseghian, right, chats with Alabama coach Paul "Bear" Bryant prior to the 1973 Sugar Bowl. Notre Dame topped Alabama 24-23 to claim the national championship. South Bend Tribune File Photo

College Football's Sleeping Giant Has Awakened

By Eric Hansen

Decades after Ara Parseghian walked away from coaching, the only accessories he needed to watch Notre Dame football games were a legal pad and a pen.

He scribbled notes, charted plays, dissected strategy — essentially coached the games from his sofa.

That is until Notre Dame football was awakened in 2012.

A No. 1 ranking and a chance to witness national championship No. 12 in the program's storied history wasn't enough to coax the 89-year-old ND coaching icon from his winter home in Marco Island, Fla., across Alligator Alley to Sun Life Stadium in Miami Gardens.

But it did prompt a change in his game-day behavior.

"I'm not going to use the notepad," he said, just days before ND's clash with No. 2 Alabama in the second-to-last BCS National Championship Game on Jan. 7. "I'm going to be a cheerleader and cheer like hell instead. Notre Dame has a coach who I believe in."

In the wee hours of the morning on Jan. 8, third-year Notre Dame head football coach Brian Kelly had a lot fewer believers than just hours before.

Though the ferocity and completeness of Alabama's 42-14 throttling of the Irish ended a dream season, it may have fueled another.

"We've got to get physically stronger, continue to close the gap there," Kelly said moments after the Crimson Tide hoisted the crystal football. "Now our guys

clearly know what (a championship team) looks like. Measure yourself against that, and I think it was pretty clear across the board what we have to do.

"I don't want to minimize the fact that we have made incredible strides to get to this point. Now it's pretty clear what we need to do to get over the top."

It's not the blueprint that's broken. In fact, Notre Dame now matches Alabama's SEC style. It's the substance that needs to continue to evolve.

The days that followed the title-game loss proved to be even more challenging in terms of reaching that end.

Kelly interviewed for the head coaching position with the NFL's Philadelphia Eagles the day after the loss to Alabama, then spent 3½ days detached from the story, his players and his recruits before Notre Dame announced on Jan. 12 that he would be, in fact, coming back to ND for Year 4. The Eagles job eventually went to Kelly's friend (but no relation), Oregon coach Chip Kelly.

Brian Kelly lost linebacker recruit Alex Anzalone in the interim. The top 30 prospect nationally, from Wyomissing, Pa., flipped to Florida during the silence. He had been projected to compete to become All-American Manti Te'o's successor.

Speaking of Te'o, four days after the Kelly story lost its legs, the flip side of Manti Mania surfaced in a piece by Deadspin.com. It not only dominated sports head-

The statue of Lou Holtz outside Notre Dame Stadium sits covered with leis draped around the coach and players and at its base following Notre Dame's win against Michigan on Sept. 22. Fans wore the leis to the game to show their support for Notre Dame linebacker Manti Te'o after the Irish senior lost his girlfriend and grandmother. South Bend Tribune/ROBERT FRANKLIN

lines for days, the story bled into places like Access Hollywood, TMZ, Inside Edition and *People* magazine.

Notre Dame athletic director Jack Swarbrick was the first to portray Te'o as a victim in a cruel hoax instead of a co-conspirator, as Deadspin had strongly suggested earlier on Jan. 16. The very public debate simmered and shifted as additional pieces of information floated into the storyline.

We decided to include the original articles about Te'o, complete in their original form, because we feel it helps tell the story of the season, even though it's clear now that the person he had come to know as Lennay Kekua was someone playing the role in a con, and she didn't die from leukemia on Sept. 12, as we and later so many others reported.

As for the bigger picture of where Notre Dame football goes from here, there is inspiration for the Irish to be found in Alabama's rise.

Nick Saban, the head coach of college football's newest dynasty, had days like Kelly experienced on Jan. 7 on his own way up.

Saban lost to hyphenated underdog Louisiana-Monroe — in Tuscaloosa, no less — in year one of his regime, and ended that 2007 season with an invite to the Independence Bowl in Shreveport, La. — not exactly a touchstone of an ascending team.

The next year, Alabama ripped off 12 straight wins, only to lose to Florida 31-20 in the SEC Championship Game. The Tide then got run by Utah in the Sugar Bowl, 31-17.

But Saban never scrapped the process, never stopped believing in the process or stopped pushing the process along. Neither, likely, will Kelly.

"I couldn't be more proud of especially my seniors," Kelly said. "What they have done in a very short period of time to help elevate our program back into the spotlight, competing for a national championship, can never be repaid.

"Now it's up to those that return to take it one more step, and we saw that that step needs to happen."

The step that took place in 2012 saw the Irish finish No. 4 in the final AP poll, their highest season-ending ranking since 1993 — the year Irish starting quarterback Everett Golson was born.

Manti Mania gripped the nation, not just for Te'o's courage for fighting through personal tragedy — his grandmother actually did pass on Sept. 11 — but for pushing a team that started the year unranked back into national prominence and setting a standard for future Irish teams to follow.

How Te'o's legacy is framed for the long term has yet to play out, but he did collect the most votes ever for a pure defensive player in the Heisman Trophy voting while finishing second to Texas A&M quarterback Johnny Manziel. He also became the most decorated college football player ever in winning seven major national awards, including the Lombardi, Walter Camp and Maxwell awards.

What's also very real is that this Notre Dame team showed academics and good football really aren't mutually exclusive, that it's okay to dream big and that maybe there's enough magic and talent to make another run to the title game next January in Pasadena, Calif.

Above all, it's a team that brought the Notre Dame family back together. It's toughness, its stars in the trenches, its ability to overcome. It wasn't just the winning. It was the way this Irish team won.

Until the Alabama game, it reminded Notre Dame's past players of their own teams. After the shell shock of Jan. 7 fades, it probably will again.

The foundation is too strong, the team's resolve too high, the coach's recruiting too relentless for this all to slip gently into the darkness. Make no mistake, one of college football's sleeping giants has awakened.

Now it's up to the Irish to climb another wall of adversity in the offseason and keep Parseghian's legal pad and pen out of commission for good. ∎

Manti Te'o walks off the field following Notre Dame's loss to Alabama in the BCS National Championship Game. It was the final game of the senior's storied Notre Dame career. South Bend Tribune/ROBERT FRANKLIN

5

QUARTERBACK

EVERETT GOLSON

The ascent of a signal caller

By Eric Hansen • August 18, 2012

In what turned out to be a transformative encounter with former Notre Dame quarterback Tony Rice, Everett Golson never did find out about Rice's first collegiate play of significance. For the record, it unfolded 25 autumns ago, the sophomore from Woodruff, S.C., summoned into a game against Pitt on the road, just after halftime, because of a broken collarbone to then-starter Terry Andrysiak. Rice broke the huddle, strode toward the line and promptly readied himself to take the snap...

From an offensive guard.

"I think that's one of the stories he left out," said Golson, ND's current depth-chart surger at quarterback.

When the sophomore from Myrtle Beach, S.C., stopped laughing, he volunteered that he did the very same thing during spring practice four months ago, back when he was the long shot in a protracted four-quarterback audition to be the starter this fall.

By the time Golson and Rice met, the 6-foot, 185-pound sophomore was dramatically ascending.

In the end, it might not have mattered whether semi-incumbent Tommy Rees had been suspended

for the Sept. 1 season opener against Navy or if junior Andrew Hendrix had become a master improviser on broken plays or if freshman Gunner Kiel had pulled an Evelyn Wood on the playbook.

"I think the Everett we saw last year was playing because he was just having fun. He was just playing around," Irish All-America linebacker Manti Te'o observed. "This Everett has that same kind of energy, but it's more focused. 'Man, I'm going to win games. I'm going to help our team win.'

"This Everett is very critical of himself. He's very critical of the way he plays. And it's humbling, because he comes up to me and he asks me, 'What do you see? How's the offense looking? How am I doing?' He's very determined to be the very best quarterback he can."

How Golson got to this point, charging hard from the back of the pack to become the unconfirmed No. 1 option at QB for the opener in Ireland, comprises seemingly a million little shifts that together add up to a quantum leap.

But it started in a dark place with a promise to himself. And by the time Rice counseled Golson on how to handle the pressures on the outside, the

Everett Golson looks downfield during Notre Dame's 38-0 win over Wake Forest on Nov. 17. Golson threw for a season-high 346 yards as the Irish notched their 11th win. South Bend Tribune/JAMES BROSHER

Everett Golson takes part in Notre Dame's August 30 practice in Dublin, Ireland, before the season opener against Navy. The sophomore, who did not play in 2011, beat out Tommy Rees and Andrew Hendrix to earn the starting job behind center. South Bend Tribune/SANTIAGO FLORES

attention, the expectations and the disappointments, Golson was ready to hear them and apply them.

"He kind of put everything in perspective," Golson said of Rice.

But not before Golson did himself.

Midway through the 2011 season, Golson and Hendrix were competing for a minor role in the Irish offense—the change-up quarterback.

It was a concept Kelly began toying with, at least in the meeting room, the previous spring after talking to Urban Meyer, who tag-teamed then-freshman Tim Tebow with senior Chris Leak in a national title run at Florida in 2006. But Kelly was slow to employ the concept in a game in the fall of '11, and had a tough time separating Hendrix and Golson as the top candidate for that role—until Golson sort of did it for him at midseason.

He began to struggle in the classroom, more of a sign of lack of maturity than anything else, and his attention to detail when it came to being on time and focused for meetings, for example, was far from perfect.

"I can admit I wasn't the best at that," he said.

Golson then was demoted to scout team for the remainder of the season. His job, at that point, was to learn the opposing team's plays and run their offenses in practice against ND's No. 1 defense. The decline, though, started to gain traction all the way back in August training camp in 2011.

"I thought I was ready to compete for the starting spot," said Golson, the sixth-most prolific TD thrower in U.S. high school history. "Going through fall camp, I kind of saw my reps go down a little bit. I was a little bit discouraged at first.

"It kind of humbled me. Now that I look back at it, I'm glad I went down to the scout team, 'cause it made me realize I have to start at ground zero and work my way back up."

First, though, came the doubts about whether he had made the right college decision, whether he'd ever be the right fit in Kelly's offense and whether he'd ever get the chance to prove it.

"I think every player has that experience," Golson said. "It's not about whether you have it, it's what you do with it. And I think me going through that has obviously helped me to mature and helped me focus in and confirm—this is really what I want to do.

"So I had to put myself in the best position to do it."

That process started with Golson trying to learn the Irish offense on his own while the scout-team QB. He'd head to the film room by himself after practice and watch what Rees, Hendrix and since-transferred QB Dayne Crist had done at the other end of the practice field.

"It was kind of on a basic level, because I didn't

really understand it totally," Golson said of his learning curve. "But at least I was getting a little bit familiar with it. So that helped me out a lot."

So did Kelly's promotion of safeties coach Chuck Martin to offensive coordinator, and Golson's commitment to learning to throw with touch on shorter routes, and his study of shorter quarterbacks—such as New Orleans Saints star Drew Brees and Seattle Seahawks QB Russell Wilson—to decipher how best to find throwing lanes over and around a towering offensive line.

The confidence that had helped him win two high school state titles in football and one as an all-state point guard in basketball re-germinated.

"Once a player has their confidence, you cannot mess with them," said Te'o, who tried to encourage all four QBs during the summer. "(That player) is going to be special."

From Kelly's standpoint, the ascendance was a gradual process.

"I think (it was) the individual meetings during spring," Kelly said of the turning point for him. "And then how he handled his academics in the summer and all those little things. He's built trust along the way.

"And then you build trust when I'm around you every day. This camp obviously was a big proving ground for him, and he's doing well."

Just as important as the things Golson changed were two things he did not.

Music remained his outlet to decompress, and he often would stop at the ND band room on his walk to ND's football facility to play the piano.

He also composes music and plays a variety of other instruments—all without the ability to actually read music.

"I play by ear," he said, "and I think that helps me when I have to improvise in football."

The other constant he held onto was throwing the football without trying to locate the laces. In fact, he spins the football to avoid the laces. It's a practice that's not unprecedented in college and pro football, but certainly rare.

"I've always been like that," Golson said. "It just felt comfortable to me."

Kelly didn't try to convince him otherwise. What he did coax Golson to do was to was to crank up the volume, to be a presence, to assert his command—a point Golson ran with to such an extreme late last week that he was hoarse when he spoke with the media.

"I think it was something that was always in me," he said about commanding a presence, "but I was scared to really show it. Now that the opportunity has presented itself, you have to really step up and be that leader."

Rice told him that too. He also told him how hard you have to work in the present, now matter how decorated your past.

And their pre-ND pasts were eerily similar. Both led their football teams to two South Carolina state titles each. Both were standout hoops players as well.

Rice, in fact, teamed with former Irish coach Lou Holtz, fellow QB Kent Graham and ex-Irish basketball player Jeff Peters to reach the semifinals of the 666-team intracampus Bookstore Basketball Tournament the spring before Rice took the Irish football team to its most recent national title (1988).

Golson aimed higher and initially hoped to play for coach Mike Brey's varsity squad. He's settled in as a pickup player, though the frequency and intensity of which he'd prefer not to share with Kelly.

"Basketball's still my first love," he said.

But football is where he dreams now. Big dreams. And Rice encouraged him to do so. Yet, even now, as his reality is merging with those dreams, he goes back to the dark place where the climb started.

Back to working like he's still fourth string.

"What helped me tremendously was grinding in the film room," Golson said, "being persistent, for long hours, knowing I have to get this in order for me to have a chance to be the starting quarterback.

"I'm definitely not where I want to be. I've seen growth, but obviously, I have a long, long way to go." ■

SEPTEMBER 1, 2012 • DUBLIN, IRELAND

NOTRE DAME 50, NAVY 10

A Wee Bit O' Dominance

Golson, Irish stay poised, rout Navy

By Bob Wieneke

Throughout most of Saturday's game against Navy, Notre Dame quarterback Everett Golson displayed a good dose of poise.

That show of composure in his first career start extended into the postgame press conference as Golson fielded questions from American and European reporters following the 2012 season opener, which was played at Aviva Stadium.

With head coach Brian Kelly and linebacker Manti Te'o joining him at a table, Golson was answering a question when a reporter interrupted to ask Kelly a question.

Flustered? Nope.

Golson deferred to the head coach before flashing a million-euro grin.

Golson and the Irish had a lot to smile about Saturday following a 50-10 smashing of Navy. Golson certainly wasn't the offensive star, but as a first-time starter at quarterback, he was going to be front and center, win or lose.

The Myrtle Beach, S.C., product was an efficient 12-of-18 passing with a touchdown and an interception, but that was more than good enough for the Irish, who brought to Ireland a punishing running game that produced 293 net yards and an opportunistic defense that forced four turnovers. And they left Europe with a 1-0 record.

"I thought he managed the game," Kelly said of Golson. "I think he would probably take one decision back—where he threw an interception."

The interception came with the Irish leading 20-0 late in the first half.

The Irish offense would not touch the ball the rest of the half, giving Golson plenty of time to let the turnover fester in his mind.

But it never did.

Notre Dame's dominating defense made its presence felt in the season-opening rout of Navy. Defensive end Kapron Lewis-Moore celebrates a stop, maybe realizing that his championship dreams might finally be in reach after five years in the Irish program. South Bend Tribune/SANTIAGO FLORES

Instead, he completed 6 of 8 passes in the second half before leaving late in the third quarter with the big lead intact and the win securely in place.

"The great thing about Everett is he figures it out," Kelly said. "He's not going to make the same mistake twice. Other than that, I was really pleased with the leadership, the ability to get in the right plays and keep our offense moving."

"I think I was comfortable," said Golson, a sophomore who did not play last season. "Coming into this game, the main thing was everybody is going to make mistakes, but you just have to relax. You're going to make mistakes, but make them going full-speed."

It didn't take long for the Irish offense to get going full-speed. A running game that was without 1,000-yard rusher Cierre Wood, who was suspended the first two games for a violation of team rules, adopted Kelly's next-man-in philosophy.

In this case it was the tag-team of running back-turned-wide receiver-turned running back Theo Riddick, and sophomore George Atkinson. Riddick carried 19 times for 107 yards and two TDs while Atkinson provided 99 yards and a pair of scores on nine carries.

Riddick's 11-yard touchdown run on the first possession of the season put the Irish up 6-0, the blip coming when Nick Tausch missed the extra point.

After the Irish offensive line bullied the Midshipmen, it was the defense's turn. Navy moved to the ND 30 and, with a fourth-and-1, went for it, providing an early key moment. That key moment went Notre Dame's way.

ND's Manti Te'o and Dan Fox stuffed Navy quarterback Trey Miller for no gain, and a couple minutes later, it was 13-0 after Atkinson burst through the line, moved right and then zipped left and into the end zone.

The rest of the half was largely Notre Dame, the highlight coming when ND defensive end Stephon Tuitt did his best Usain Bolt imitation when he picked up a fumble caused by Ishaq Williams and sprinted 77 yards to make it 27-0.

Irish running back Theo Riddick celebrates after one of his two touchdown runs against Navy. The former wide receiver racked up 107 yards on 19 carries in the season opener against the Midshipmen. South Bend Tribune/SANTIAGO FLORES

"He was telling everybody about it too," Kelly quipped. "Trust me."

The big lead built, Kelly was able to put his trust in his running game, and force Navy out of its comfort zone. Granted, Miller is considered a serviceable passer, but Navy's running game is its money-maker.

"We fell behind," said Navy coach Ken Niumatalolo, "and got out of the nature of who we are as a football team."

After the Irish went up 40-10 late in the third quarter, Golson donned a red hat and was able to watch the final 15-plus minutes from the sidelines as the Irish reserves maintained the rout.

Were there reasons for concern? Yes, particularly in the secondary where cornerbacks Bennett Jackson and KeiVarae Russell were making their first career starts. Miller threw for 192 yards and a touchdown and found a number of wide-open receivers. Kelly chose to focus on the positives.

"I thought they did some great things," said Kelly, who is 2-1 in openers at Notre Dame. "I'm really excited about their ability to go out there and compete. The learning experience that they got today was so big for us as we move now onto our next challenge."

Special teams too provided some hiccups for the Irish, who were ranked 24th this week in the coaches' poll. Tausch missed an extra point and another extra point went awry when the snap went through holder Ben Turk's hands.

Still, it was a win, something the Irish couldn't say last year following the opening weekend when they lost to South Florida at home. It also concluded a successful trip to Dublin for the Irish, who boarded a plane and headed back over the Atlantic soon after the game.

"We're definitely going to miss it," Te'o said, "but it's time to get back to work." ■

Sophomore defensive end Stephon Tuitt races 77 yards for the end zone after picking up a second-quarter Navy fumble. His score gave Notre Dame an insurmountable 27-0 lead en route to a season-opening trouncing of the Midshipmen. South Bend Tribune/ SANTIAGO FLORES

SEPTEMBER 8, 2012 · SOUTH BEND, INDIANA
NOTRE DAME 20, PURDUE 17

Rees Steps In, Rescues ND

Backup leads late drive to top Purdue

By Eric Hansen

By the time the brief cascade of boos had faded and sophomore kicker Kyle Brindza was celebrating his improbable ascent to a Notre Dame moment, Brian Kelly knew.

The Irish head football coach knew that all of his sometimes-painful introspection in the offseason, his readjusting his coaching template, his mending with the players he had become too disconnected from had turned out to be more than potent rhetoric after all.

They were the threads that ran through every pivotal moment of 22nd-ranked Notre Dame's 20-17 escape from rival Purdue Saturday at ND Stadium and allowed the Irish to sidestep a trap door into irrelevance two weeks into the season, in a game when some of its biggest stars finished the game as spectators.

"Our guys kept fighting," Kelly said. "The next guy came in and battled."

If the identical circumstances had surfaced late last season, there might not have been enough cohesiveness and resolve to overcome Purdue's surprising smash-mouth bravado. Saturday it became a season-saving tourniquet.

Defensive end Kapron Lewis-Moore missed all but the first series of the game with a calf strain. ND's most experienced and valuable player in a fledgling secondary, safety Jamoris Slaughter, missed the entire second half with a shoulder injury.

Lewis-Moore's backup, freshman Sheldon Day, left with dehydration. Outside linebacker Ishaq Williams, one week after a breakout game, exited with an elbow injury.

And when the Irish needed some offensive magic in the final 2:05 of the game, All-America tight end Tyler Eifert (concussion) and most dangerous deep receiving threat, DaVaris Daniels (ankle sprain) weren't available.

Irish running back Theo Riddick hurdles Purdue cornerback Josh Johnson during Notre Dame's hard-fought 20-17 victory over its Indiana rivals. South Bend Tribune/JAMES BROSHER

Junior quarterback Tommy Rees was, and his insertion into the game on ND's final offensive possession was in part dictated by a hand injury starter Everett Golson suffered on the previous drive. But Rees' moxie was even more of a factor, even if his only meaningful practice reps since last spring came this week.

"I thought that was a really good decision by their head coach," Purdue coach Danny Hope said. "That was a pressure situation and certainly would have been a tough assignment for a rookie quarterback.

"I was kind of excited about the idea of maybe having a rookie quarterback in there on the last drive. I thought that may have given us an opportunity to get after him some and get ourselves in position to win."

Kelly in late July suspended Rees for the season opener with Navy, but the timing and circumstances of the suspension led Kelly to commit to using only Golson and junior Andrew Hendrix in team drills.

Rees had three practices and a walk-through to de-rust himself. And by week's end, Kelly was a believer.

What turned out to be Golson's final possession of the day ended with the quarterback fumbling at the ND 15-yard line, with Purdue cornerback Josh Johnson forcing and recovering it at the 3:24 mark of the fourth quarter.

That set up the tying TD for the Boilermakers (1-1), who converted a fourth-and-10 situation into a 15-yard score from Caleb TerBush to Antavian Edison.

"He had trouble gripping the ball," Kelly said of Golson, who accounted for 204 of ND's 207 total yards in Saturday's first half. "I think he could have probably still have gone.

"This is not going to be an excuse for Everett that he's pulled out because of an injury. We also made the decision with the flow of the game that Tommy could come in there and manage our two minute (drill), and he did a great job.

"I will further say, there is no quarterback controversy. Everett Golson's our starter. He will start against

Michigan State. We know we have assets at that position with Andrew Hendrix and Tommy Rees."

That the Irish will be taking on the Spartans next Saturday night with an unblemished record couldn't have happened without Brindza, the sophomore whose second career field goal untied the game with nine seconds left.

His first collegiate attempt, a 40-yarder late in the first quarter of a scoreless tie, sailed badly to the left. His game-winner, a 27-yarder, was dead center. Forty-eight hours earlier he was the backup.

But senior Nick Tausch suffered a groin strain and pushed Brindza into the spotlight.

"Kyle had to step in," Kelly said. "That's why I'm so proud of my guys. Next man in. Went in and got the job done."

And how did Brindza feel about it? Brindza and both Irish quarterbacks were among the players requested for postgame interviews by the media but weren't allowed to do so.

Rees did a brief TV interview on the field, but his loudest talking came courtesy of his right arm.

George Atkinson's 32-yard kickoff return set the Irish up on their own 35 with 2:05 left and every timeout already burned.

Rees' first pass resulted in a defensive holding penalty. His second, an overthrow, coaxed boos from the stands.

"I was a bit surprised," Irish linebacker Manti Te'o said of the crowd reaction. "But I think Tommy knew it didn't really matter, because he knew what was most important is that the guys out there on the field and the guys on the sideline trusted him and had confidence in his ability to make plays."

Two plays later, Rees did in a big way, connecting with John Goodman on sort of a jump ball for a 10-yard gain on third and six. It was Goodman's first catch of the season.

Two incomplete passes later, Rees converted another third down. This one was a 21-yard catch and run to Robby Toma and it pushed the Irish to the Purdue 20.

An 11-yard run by Theo Riddick, ND's longest rush of the game, got ND inside the 10.

Rees finished the drive 3-of-8 for 35 yards, but he got his first win as a relief quarterback after going 0-4 in his previous non-starting cameos in which Rees had thrown at least one pass. Rees was 12-4 as a starter before being displaced by Golson.

"That's what I knew about him and his makeup, his moxie, his mental toughness," Kelly beamed. "Does he have all of the elite skills? No, but he's a gamer. He'll do anything. Those guys in that locker room will go to the wall for him. They'll do anything, because he's a great teammate.

"He's working the whole game, talking to Everett about different looks, different coverages. He's the consummate teammate. That's why those guys in the locker room are pretty happy."

Kelly was happiest that none of the injuries appeared to be long-term at first glance. He's also happy that his defense lived up to its preseason hopes for a second straight week and that the secondary that looked so shaky against Navy showed growth against a conventional offense.

But the big picture is fuzzy beyond Kelly knowing what his team's heart looks like now.

Golson's second start, for instance, looked more like a first—though he did manage to go 21-of-31 for 289 yards and one TD without an interception. But he was also sacked five times, and not all of those were the offensive line's fault.

He saw the defensive template Saturday that he'll see every week until he can make defenses pay for doing so, a stacked box daring him to pass and making running the ball tortuous.

"Offensively, you know, we're evolving," Kelly said. "We knew we were going to be challenged to throw the football today, and we were." ■

Irish wide receiver John Goodman makes a critical third-down catch to keep alive Notre Dame's final drive of the game against Purdue. Moments later, kicker Kyle Brindza sealed the comeback win with a clutch 27-yard field goal. South Bend Tribune/JAMES BROSHER

SEPTEMBER 15, 2012 • EAST LANSING, MICHIGAN
NOTRE DAME 20, MICHIGAN STATE 3

Another (Big) Step For Irish

Defense drives ND to road win

By Eric Hansen

They were 15 minutes from the biggest perceptual counterpunch since a 2005 near-miss prematurely launched Notre Dame football into the notion that it was back.

Fifteen minutes removed from ending a nine-game losing streak to Top 10 teams. Fifteen minutes removed from the first 3-0 start since Tyrone Willingham's 2002 squad made a faux run at national prominence.

And just when the familiar fourth-quarter fade was all queued up, the 20th-ranked Irish went beyond finding the required magic to finish the job against 10th-ranked Michigan State. They found the accelerator and stomped on it hard in a 20-3 uprising.

An 84-yard, clock-killing drive that culminated in a 29-yard field goal from Irish sophomore and Michigan native Kyle Brindza for a 17-3 Irish advantage was followed by another smothering surge by an ND defense that out-smashmouthed the Spartans from the opening possession.

Brindza would tack on a 47-yarder, the longest of his fledgling career with 3:18 left. The Spartan offense could only flail at reducing the final margin and the magnitude of a loss that effectively knocked the Big Ten out of the national title conversation just three weeks into the season.

"The most important thing is that our defense continues to be the group that we had committed to in building when we started this process," Irish head coach Brian Kelly said. "And they're starting to get to that level that can play against anybody."

In the end, the Irish recorded four sacks against the team that came into the weekend leading the nation with zero given up. The Irish limited the Spartans (2-1) to 50 rushing yards on 25 carries a year after

Notre Dame defensive lineman Tony Springmann, left, celebrates a defensive stop. The Irish held the nation's 10th-ranked team to just three points. South Bend Tribune/JAMES BROSHER

28

squelching them for 29 on 23 carries.

The three points were the fewest yielded to a top 10 team since a 28-3 Cotton Bowl romp over Texas A&M on Jan. 1, 1993 and the fewest against a top 10 team in the road since coach Ara Parseghian's 1966 national champs took down USC 51-0 on Nov. 26 of that year.

Senior linebacker Manti Te'o transcended a tragic week with an inspired performance that saw him climb past Mike Kovaleski and into the No. 6 spot on ND's all-time tackle list and spearhead the biggest upset of his career.

He finished with 12 tackles and two pass breakups in a game dedicated to his grandmother, who died Tuesday, and girlfriend who died less than 24 hours later. Te'o's girlfriend, Lennay Kekua, had been battling leukemia and having some success in treatment when her recovery took a sudden and cruel twist.

"I'll miss them both," Te'o said after the game. "But I know I'll see them both again someday."

"The entire defense is his family, because during this tough time all he wanted to do was be at practice with his teammates," Kelly said of Te'o. "Given all the distractions and tragedy to have to deal with, he went and played really good football, too.

"He's so strong for everybody, that when he was in a time everybody wanted to help him out. I've never seen that kind of dynamic amongst a team and a group of players. It's a pretty close locker room."

Te'o's childhood friend, senior wide receiver Robby Toma, also rose to the occasion with a team-high five receptions for 58 yards.

Irish sophomore quarterback Everett Golson's numbers, meanwhile, looked forgettable without context. He finished 14-of-32 for 178 yards and one touchdown in the worst statistical game of his young career and easily the most impressive when it came to hinting at him being the long-term answer at the position.

After the Irish committed an illegal procedure penalty on its first play from scrimmage and had to call a timeout before getting off the second, Golson settled the

Notre Dame defensive end Stephon Tuitt lays a hit on Michigan State quarterback Andrew Maxwell. The Irish sacked Maxwell four times on the night. South Bend Tribune/JAMES BROSHER

offense down and got the Irish into the end zone on their next possession.

A 36-yard scoring pass to senior John Goodman with 10:34 left in the opening quarter gave the Irish a 7-0 lead and accounted for the first offensive touchdown the Spartans have given up this season.

Golson added a six-yard run on a scramble with 10:50 left in the first half for a 14-0 Irish command. But the most impressive drive ended with a field goal in the fourth quarter.

"It was big, because he needed to be in this atmosphere," Kelly said. "He needed to be on the road in this kind of great collegiate atmosphere and a very difficult football team that you're playing. He needed these kinds of experiences and he's going to get more of them."

MSU's punt team pinned Notre Dame at its own 4 with 13:49 left. The Irish running game then came alive, with Cierre Wood going nine yards on first down and 26 more on second.

Wood also helped the Irish convert a fourth-and-1 from with Spartan 37 later in the drive with an eight yard jaunt. The Irish burned 6:35 in the 84-yard, 12-play drive that was capped by Brindza's 29-yard field goal.

"The ability to run the football late in the game proved to probably be the deciding factor," Kelly said. ∎

Left: Notre Dame linebacker Manti Te'o points to the sky in the moments after Notre Dame's 20-3 win. Te'o's grandmother and girlfriend both passed away in the days leading up to the game. Above: Notre Dame athletic director Jack Swarbrick greets players on the field after the game. The win ended Notre Dame's nine-game losing streak against Top 10-ranked teams. South Bend Tribune/ JAMES BROSHER

SEPTEMBER 22, 2012 · SOUTH BEND, INDIANA
NOTRE DAME 13, MICHIGAN 6

Secondary Steals Spotlight

Irish defense superb in win over U-M

By Eric Hansen

They lingered in the late-October-esque weather, donned leis honoring Notre Dame's latest and least-conventional Heisman Trophy conversation piece, and singing until the Notre Dame Stadium ushers coaxed them toward the exits.

It was a strange concoction of belief and disbelief that mingled in the aftermath of the 11th-ranked ND football team's latest step into the BCS conversation, a 13-6 subduing of 18th-ranked Michigan on Saturday night that teemed with statistical strangeness and karmic plot twists.

Of all the hairpin curves, though, that saturated a victory likely to boost the Irish (4-0) into the top 10 of the Associated Press poll for the first time since 2006, the most stunning was the Irish secondary flexing its muscle and ruining both Michigan quarterback Denard Robinson's flailing Heisman

hopes and his 22nd birthday.

Two freshman defensive backs, KeiVarae Russell and Nicky Baratti, accounted for two of the six turnovers the Irish defense forced. They each had an interception. First-year starting cornerback Bennett Jackson also had one, along with a team-high nine tackles and a fumble recovery.

The soul of the defense, though, remains senior middle linebacker Manti Te'o, whose own numbers, and those by the Irish defense as a whole, have him in the periphery of national player of the year patter.

Roughly a week and a half removed from the heartbreak of losing his grandmother and girlfriend, Te'o responded with eight tackles, including one for loss, and the second and third interceptions of his career. The ND student section and several thousand other Irish fans wore leis

Quarterback Tommy Rees entered in the second quarter in relief of a struggling Everett Golson, who had thrown two picks. Rees was solid and error-free in the win, finishing 8-of-11 for 115 yards passing and scoring on a short run. South Bend Tribune/JAMES BROSHER

in support of the Laie, Hawaii, native.

"That lei, for me, it represents family," he said. "It doesn't represent me. It represents family. It represents everybody sticking together and everybody realizing what's important in life, and that's families."

Overall, the Irish have stuck together to the point of surpassing the 1988 national champs' scoring defense performance through four games. The 2012 incarnation has given up 36 points a third of the way through the season. The 1988 squad yielded 41 at the same juncture.

You have to go all the way back to 1975—Dan Devine's first Irish squad—to find a stingier start. That group held Boston College, Purdue, Northwestern and Michigan State collectively to 20 points.

The lowest-scoring game in the series since an 11-3 Irish win in 1909 was not without its flaws and anxious moments for third-year head coach Brian Kelly. And most of them occurred on offense.

Kelly, in fact, relieved starting quarterback Everett Golson at the 6:10 mark of the second quarter and the Irish laboring with a 3-0 lead. Still, even, with junior tag-teamer Tommy Rees at the joystick, Notre Dame was sitting on 140 yards in total offense at the end of the third quarter and finished with a season-low 239.

The Irish also labored to run the ball 94 yards on 31 carries against the nation's 104th-ranked rush defense (out of 120 FBS schools).

"What I was most pleased with our offense was the ability to close out a game," Kelly said.

That they did. Two clock-killing drives in the fourth quarter ended in a 39-yard Kyle Brindza field goal and in the victory formation deep in Michigan territory.

A 38-yard pass to Tyler Eifert on third and 4 from ND's 31 with 2:35 left was the play that allowed the Irish to run out the clock. It was Eifert's first reception since suffering a concussion late in the Purdue game two weeks ago and the 99th of his career.

Rees finished 8-of-11 for 115 yards without an interception and accounted for the game's only touchdown on his first career touchdown run, from two yards out

Notre Dame's Louis Nix III (left) and Stephon Tuitt (7) pressure Michigan quarterback Denard Robinson. Robinson—who entered the 2012 season as a favorite to win the Heisman Trophy—was sacked three times and threw four interceptions. South Bend Tribune/ **JAMES BROSHER**

late in the second quarter.

He entered the game at a time when the teams had combined for six interceptions and just eight completions. Golson was 3-of-8 for 30 yards with two interceptions.

Said Rees, "(Golson) was real supportive. He was talking to me about some things he was seeing. He couldn't have been more positive."

"Everett's our starter," Kelly insisted after the game. "He was not as comfortable as I would have liked. He just needs to settle down a little bit. He'll have a week (ahead), where he doesn't have three exams and four papers."

Michigan's Robinson too can hope for a better week ahead. He did have enough yards (228) to pass Chad Henne to become Michigan's leader in total offense, but he accounted for five of the six Michigan turnovers—four interceptions and a fumble.

Running back Vincent Smith threw the other interception.

It was a stark reversal to last year's game, in which Michigan won the turnover battle, 5-0. This time it was 6-2, pushing Kelly's career record to 116-12 when his teams have fewer turnovers than the opponents.

"We have to do a better job," Michigan coach Brady Hoke said. "And it starts with me." ■

Left: The Irish secondary starred in the win over Michigan, so it was only appropriate that cornerback Josh Atkinson celebrated with the Notre Dame student section after the game. Above: Linebacker Manti Te'o howls with delight as the clock runs out on a masterful Notre Dame defensive performance against Michigan. South Bend Tribune/JAMES BROSHER

7
DEFENSIVE END
STEPHON TUITT
Sultan of Sack growing into his high ceiling
By Eric Hansen • September 29, 2012

On the Wednesday before Stephon Tuitt rocketed into college football's mainstream, he posted a sort of reverse help wanted ad on his Twitter account. "Are there any local farms around South Bend, Indiana? I would love to help participate in the everyday activities," the Notre Dame sophomore defensive end wrote.

What read like a prank, and wasn't specific enough to eliminate offers to have Tuitt milk cows, feed pigs or clean, um, droppings of any kind, was actually quite sincere. It's Tuitt's way of thinking way ahead about ways to get better.

"What many people don't know is I met a lot of really, really big-time country offensive linemen," the Monroe, Ga., product explained. "They're kind of strong, so I thought maybe in the offseason, I might be trying to go on a farm and move some hay or do whatever they did to get stronger."

And that's the scariest part of the 6-foot-6, 303-pounder with tight end speed's game—that the confusion that pocked his otherwise promising debut season in 2011 has been replaced by both a larger knowledge base about how to play within ND's scheme and a relentless passion to touch his high ceiling...this season.

"You're shocked when you watch him run," Irish defensive coordinator Bob Diaco said. "He really runs like a little guy. He's got a lot of foot action. He can change directions. He's an excellent athlete. He can bend and twist.

"So he's got a unique blend of tangible traits coupled with...that intangible element of effort and intensity and passion in that he just loves to play football."

Michigan probably wouldn't have minded if Tuitt had been busy with his new farming avocation last Saturday night.

Tuitt, star linebacker Manti Te'o, and a makeshift secondary that plays like it has years—not days—together, had dismantled a Michigan State offense in a national showcase the weekend before. But Michigan, with perhaps the most electric offensive player in the nation—quarterback Denard Robinson—was viewed as the real litmus test.

Robinson alone amassed 446 yards against the Irish last season, 502 in 2010. But this Irish defense "Alabama-ed" the Wolverine offense, giving

Stephon Tuitt celebrates after sacking Cougars quarterback Riley Nelson during Notre Dame's Oct. 20 win over BYU. The sophomore had two sacks on the day. South Bend Tribune/JAMES BROSHER

The Los Angeles Coliseum crowd embraces Stephon Tuitt after Notre Dame's 22-13 win over USC on Nov. 24. South Bend Tribune/JAMES BROSHER

up eight fewer points and just 30 more total yards (299) than the nation's No. 1 team did in Michigan's season opener.

Te'o then spilled into the Heisman Trophy conversation and players like safety Zeke Motta, outside linebacker Prince Shembo and Tuitt became part of the national buzz. In fact, the committee for the Chuck Bednarik Award, which honors the nation's top defensive player, added Tuitt this week to its watch list, which includes just three other sophomores.

In the Michigan game, Tuitt picked up his sixth solo sack of the season, which has him tied for the most in the nation. It also eclipsed the 5.5 South Florida defector Aaron Lynch led the Irish with all of last season.

In fact, Tuitt's six total sacks would have shared the lead or outright led the Irish in sacks for the entire year in 14 of the 24 seasons dating back to ND's last national title run in 1988.

He's on pace for 18, which would obliterate New York Giants star Justin Tuck's single-season school record of 13½.

"We want to be great," said Tuitt, constantly thinking and talking team. "To be honest, I want to break the history books. I want our names to go down for things that past teams haven't done.

"With all respect to the past players who played here and were phenomenal, we have the potential to be a great defense. We just have to keep working at it to find that, be smart in our assignments and be smart in our positions."

His motivation comes from a variety of sources.

There's mom Tamara Tuitt, a deputy sheriff in the Gwinnett County (Ga.) sheriff's department, who seemingly remains the one person who can intimidate the nation's fastest-rising defensive star.

Tamara moved the family to Georgia when Stephon was 14 after obtaining her master's in criminal law. Up until that time, the family lived in Miami, which makes ND's next game—Oct. 6 against his hometown Hurricanes—extra spicy.

There's the vintage Hurricane defenses, which Tuitt isn't old enough to remember firsthand. But he's watched the ESPN *30 for 30* special and he's studied the old ND-Miami rivalry.

"Miami's defense, back in the day, was really exciting to watch," he said. "Everybody was out there like some headhunters, tracking the ball and busting people's heads down. That was exciting. I want our defense to be like that too. That's a goal."

There's Tuck, whom Tuitt has met twice in person on campus and who recently tweeted to the sophomore that Tuck wanted Tuitt to break his sack record. Tuck also owns the ND career record with 24½. With two sacks last season, Tuitt is on pace to move into the top five by season's end, with 20.

"Sacks are like an energizer," Tuitt said. "Once I get one, you can't stop. I get really excited, because over the summer I worked really hard to keep increasing my pass-rushing skills, to get some of the pressure off our defense and make some plays for them."

And then there's Te'o, whom Tuitt considers his big brother.

Te'o lost his girlfriend, Lennay Kekua, Sept. 11 to leukemia and his grandmother, Annette Santiago, the next day after a long illness. He then went out and played the two most inspired games of his career, against Michigan State and Michigan, before heading to Hawaii earlier this week to honor the loved ones who passed.

"The situation he went into was a very tragic situation, which all of us prayed for him," Tuitt said. "He was going through a hard time, but we all gave him confidence to keep going.

"At that time he may have been a little weak inside, but he never showed it. He always stayed strong. And watching him kept us going strong every day in practice and going toward Michigan, playing really hard for him. When he comes back (from Hawaii), he'll have another family that'll stay strong for him."

Strength has never been a challenge for Tuitt, inner or outer. The challenge was adding agility to his brawn and power. And playing tight end in high school and running back and tight end in 7-on-7 passing camps accelerated that part of his game.

A 77-yard fumble return by Tuitt in the Sept. 1 season-opening win against Navy more then rekindled those memories.

"I joke about it all the time," Tuitt said about making a cameo on offense for the Irish. "But we haven't talked (seriously) about that. Given the opportunity to do that, I would love to."

But he loves making history more. And that's where his mind is in his few spare moments, finding out who the faces and personalities were on the vintage Irish defenses this one is suddenly being held up to.

"I haven't seen a lot of the great defensive players here," Tuitt admitted. "I probably did, but I wouldn't have known who they were."

He wants to know now. He wants to connect with them. He wants to share their experiences and funnel it into his remarkable ascent.

Just like Tuck's words did.

"I told him I'd try my best," Tuitt said, "just go out every day and try to do what I can. I just want to have a goal to go to. Maybe that will put me out there with even more fire than I have now." ■

OCTOBER 6, 2012 • CHICAGO, ILLINOIS
NOTRE DAME 41, MIAMI 3

ND Runs Wild In Windy City

Irish offense in rhythm in rout

By Eric Hansen

They scoffed at tradition at every turn.

From the Halloween-style helmets to the insistence that the whole Catholics vs. Convicts theme was tired, fossilized and had no connection to the magic run that has suddenly pushed ninth-ranked Notre Dame into the premature national title blather.

The 41-3 splattering of former bitter rival Miami Saturday night at Solider Field wasn't about resurrections and chasing ghosts. It was about raising a new tradition.

And this time, the loud, dominating numbers put up by the Irish defense had an overwhelming offensive complement. The Irish (5-0) set new season standards in first downs (34), total offense (587 yards) and rushing yards (376), admittedly against the nation's 114th-ranked defense (out of 120).

The total offense figure in fact was the best by a Notre Dame team since Charlie Weis' first offensive juggernaut (2005). The rushing yardage total was the most since the 2000 season.

Fourth-string running back Cam McDaniel provided the final, humiliating bit of syntax in a statement game for the Irish, racking up 76 yards in total offense in a 93-yard drive that culminated with his one-yard touchdown run with 1:09 left.

"We didn't play smart enough, we didn't play disciplined enough and we didn't make enough plays, it's that simple," Miami coach Al Golden said. "Give Notre Dame a lot of credit."

All Miami (4-2) could muster in the final 69 seconds was finally pushing its rushing total (84) past its accumulation of penalty yards (76). The Hurricanes are now 11-28 since 1996 when being held under 100 yards rushing.

George Atkinson III breaks free from Miami's Kacy Rodgers II during Notre Dame's rout of the Hurricanes. The sophomore running back had a big game, gaining 123 yards on 10 carries and scoring one touchdown. South Bend Tribune/ROBERT FRANKLIN

By that time, the pregame stir that Irish No. 1 quarterback Everett Golson had committed a violation of team rules was little more than a curious afterthought. Former starter and current closer Tommy Rees did start and finish Saturday night's game, but Golson looked more like the No. 1 option than at any point this season.

The sophomore was held out all of four plays to start, then put on the most masterful performance of his five-game career. He finished 17-of-22 for 186 yards passing and ran for a career-high 51 yards—all in the first half. And, the prettiest number in coach Brian Kelly's mind, the Irish went turnover-free.

"Our team rules are pretty simple as it relates to being on time," Kelly said of the Golson mini-suspension. "It wasn't a big thing in terms of a disciplinary approach. We have high standards, and we hold all of our players to those standards.

"I want our guys to be accountable. He was accountable. He knew that he's got to do a better job communicating. He was meeting with a professor and he lost track of time."

"I thought Everett grew up today. He did some really good things throwing the football for us, managed some pressure situations very well and he had his best week of practice."

Despite a couple of scares in the opening quarter, the Irish defense settled in and put up some more pretty numbers themselves. On the very first offensive play of the game, Miami leading receiver Phillip Dorsett dropped what looked to be a sure TD pass. Later in the same drive, he did it again.

But as the game wore on, the Irish defense was more good than lucky. Dorsett, who had 191 receiving yards last weekend in a win over N.C. State and 184 the week before that against Georgia Tech, finished with one catch for six yards Saturday night.

The nation's 15th-ranked passing offense garnered a modest 201 yards, due in part to the Irish offense playing keepaway. Kelly, whose Cincinnati teams typically were at or near the bottom nationally of the time of possession stat, hogged the ball 39:08 to Miami's 20:52.

Kyle Brindza kicks one of his two second-quarter field goals during Notre Dame's 41-3 win over Miami at Chicago's Soldier Field. South Bend Tribune/ROBERT FRANKLIN

Heisman Trophy candidate Manti Te'o, ND's senior middle linebacker and emotional leader, collected a team-high 10 of ND's 50 tackles.

The 39 points allowed through five games is ND's stingiest defensive start since the 1976 team yielded 37. Compare that to the 1988 national championship team's snapshot through five games (61) and the 2002 team that is the standard in this century (64).

The Irish haven't allowed a TD in 12 quarters and are the only team in the FBS yet to yield a rushing TD in 2012.

"We're always trying to keep the points down," Te'o said. "It's something that we hope to continue. For us, it's always about going out there and dominating, doing our best to dominate in whatever fashion that is."

The most lopsided game in Shamrock Series saw Notre Dame produce two 100-yard rushers in a game for the first time in a decade. Sophomore George Atkinson III ran for 123 yards on 10 carries with a 55-yard touchdown. Resurgent senior Cierre Wood amassed 118 yards on 18 careers and two TDs. Last year's Irish leading rusher came into the game with 95 yards total on the season on 17 carries.

Golson turned into a handoff machine before turning the reins over to Rees.

"I put a lot of pressure on myself in the Michigan game," said Golson, who was pulled for Rees in the second quarter of the 13-6 Irish win on Sept. 22. "Coach Kelly and coach (offensive coordinator Chuck) Martin just told me to relax and have fun out there. I never really felt like I was having fun (against Michigan)."

The Irish rushing game went into hyperdrive in the third quarter, a period in which ND started with a 13-3 lead. Nineteen of the 21 plays in the third quarter were runs, including all 12 plays in an 86-yard scoring drive that gave the Irish a 27-3 command with 2:53 left in the period.

"They were just running all over Chicago pretty much," Irish defensive end Kapron Lewis-Moore marveled. "Give credit to the offense." ■

Irish quarterback Everett Golson evades Miami defenders. Notre Dame utilized Golson in the running game for the first time, and the sophomore gained 51 yards on six carries. South Bend Tribune/ JAMES BROSHER

41
SAFETY

MATTHIAS FARLEY

Defensive back's improbable rise solidifies secondary
By Eric Hansen • October 10, 2012

His youngest of six siblings, 18-year-old brother Silas, left home to join the New York City Ballet at age 13. His sisters, Joy and Chara, look like supermodels but are really super business women. All three of Notre Dame sophomore safety Matthias Farley's older brothers have over-stuffed trophy cases. Timon even played professional basketball in Europe.

"My parents have always been very supportive of whatever we have to do," Matthias Farley said. "My dad always joked around, 'If it's legal and you like it, do it.'"

What the Charlotte, N.C., product is doing these days is as absolutely legal, but just as improbable.

In just his fourth year of organized football, and one year removed from being a scout-team receiver at ND, Farley is the safety net on the nation's 10th-ranked pass defense and the surprise player on the country's surprise team.

Farley didn't even make the travel squad when the Irish traveled to play Stanford in Palo Alto, Calif., in 2011. He watched the game on TV back in South Bend. Four years ago, he was a soccer star on a bad Charlotte (N.C.) Christian team with absolutely no football aspirations.

"It's a crazy thing to hear or see from the outside," Farley said. "For me, sometimes you've got to take a step back and say, 'Wow, all this has happened in a very short order, but it's also happened for a reason.'

"I don't know exactly what the reason is and what will become of everything, but I know that things that have happened up to this point have led to the situation I'm in now. And I'm just trying to take that and do whatever I can do to the best of my ability."

What that looks like statistically is Farley has nine tackles and no emotional scars since taking over the No. 1 free safety spot from fifth-year senior Jamoris Slaughter just after halftime of ND's breakthrough 20-3 victory over Michigan State on Sept. 15. In that game, Slaughter tore his Achilles tendon, ending his season.

But even for Farley to be the next man in at that point, makes the "Rudy" script look a little flat.

He finally gave football a try in the late spring of

Matthias Farley breaks up a third-down pass intended for Stanford tight end Zach Ertz during Notre Dame's Oct. 13 win over Stanford. A sophomore playing just his fourth year of organized football, the safety stepped up as a key part of Notre Dame's secondary in 2012. South Bend Tribune/JAMES BROSHER

Irish safety Matthias Farley celebrates after Notre Dame stopped USC on third down as part of a goal line stand late in Notre Dame's Nov. 24 win. Farley—a scout team receiver in 2011 who ascended to a key role in the secondary—led the Irish with nine tackles against the Trojans. South Bend Tribune/JAMES BROSHER

his sophomore year after soccer season had ended. Charlotte Christian head football coach Jason Estep and several close friends won him over.

Then he lost them. He showed up in green soccer cleats for his first practice. And that wasn't the worst of it. His movements were beyond awkward as he auditioned first as a wide receiver.

"When I went out for a pass, it looked like I was swimming every time I'd go into a break," he said, "so everybody knew what I was going to do. My arms looked like I was landing jets."

Playing defense came a little more naturally, since Farley's flaw as a soccer player was getting yellow cards for being overly physical. But the growth curve was so slow and painful, Farley's brother, Nathan, had to talk him out of quitting three or four times.

So did Charlotte Christian assistant Eugene Robinson, who refused to give up on his raw pupil. And that is why Farley wears No. 41 today, as a tip of the cap to the former NFL safety who wore that number during his 15-year pro career.

By the end of his first full season of football,

Farley's junior year, there was a buzz about his potential in his new sport. North Carolina, N.C. State, Wisconsin and UCLA all offered scholarships before Notre Dame jumped in the spring of Farley's junior year.

At the time, his knowledge of Notre Dame football was limited to Knute Rockne, the Four Horseman and Rudy, but he knew all about the academic reputation. And by the end of April 2010, he committed to play at ND.

"We saw him as an under-recruited, raw talent that had outstanding ball skills," said ND head coach Brian Kelly. "We didn't have a specific position for him, because he didn't have enough of a résumé to say he was an offensive or defensive player."

Kelly tried Farley as a wide receiver last fall, then switched him to safety right after the 2011 season concluded.

By June, he was one of 12 candidates jostling for playing time at safety, and at that point was a lot closer to 12th than the top of the depth chart.

The first order of business for the 6-foot-1 safety was to lose weight.

"I was 215 pounds," said the now 200-pounder. "And I'm not tall enough to be 215 pounds."

From there it was getting the coaches to trust him, staying late and coming in early for film work, picking the brains of Slaughter and senior Zeke Motta.

And faith.

"My brother Nathan and my dad (kept) saying, 'You're there for a reason.' Farley said. "'You're going through all this stuff for a reason. You wouldn't be there if there wasn't something in it for you to learn from and develop, not just as a football player, but as a person.'

"And just knowing I had gone through a more difficult transition from an entirely different sport before gave me the confidence that, as long as I just work my tail off and try to improve each and every day and try and take to the coaching, then good things will come out of it."

By mid-August he had climbed over players with more experience, fluffier high school recruiting reps or both. And when Slaughter went down, Irish defensive coordinator Bob Diaco didn't hesitate to put yet another inexperienced defensive back on the field along with first-time starting corners, junior Bennett Jackson and freshman KeiVarae Russell.

Diaco loved Farley's speed and ability to change direction, but his demeanor of not getting flustered is what separated Farley.

That came in handy last Saturday night, when Miami wide receiver Phillip Dorsett got behind the Irish defense twice on the opening drive only to drop two seemingly sure TD passes. Farley stayed calm, made his adjustments and Dorsett—who had a combined 375 receiving yards in his two games prior to the ND clash—finished with one catch for six yards.

"We came off after that first series, 'Man they are fast,'" Farley said. "But it didn't change our assignments and what we needed to do.

"It's part of the plan. I accept that. Everything happens for a reason. So I just focus on, 'I'm here and I'm trying to live in the now and enjoy every moment I have.'" ■

OCTOBER 13, 2012 • SOUTH BEND, INDIANA
NOTRE DAME 20, STANFORD 13

ND Wins Smashmouth-Fest

Irish 'stick to the plan' for OT victory

By Eric Hansen

Brian Kelly strode out of the puddles of delirium on the water- and fan-saturated Notre Dame Stadium turf Saturday night, smelling like mud and destiny.

His hair uncharacteristically mussed up from the intermittent downpours and perhaps an elongated celebration, the third-year Notre Dame head football coach almost looked like he has been in the center of the pile that wouldn't budge inches from the goal line in yet another signature win.

In one sense, perhaps he was.

The 20-13 overtime smashmouth-fest with 17th-ranked Stanford, won by the seventh-ranked Irish, cut to the core of what Kelly hoped his team would evolve into one day, 34 months after he and ND athletic director Jack Swarbrick spent the majority of the coach's job interview talking about Kelly's hidden selling point, his

vision of winning with defense.

The Irish got just enough offense from their quarterback tag-team, this time necessitated by a late injury to starter Everett Golson, and enough push and toughness in their running game against the nation's No. 6 run defense to prolong the magic another week.

But this time they had to come from behind. ND was the last team in the FBS to trail at any point in any game this season, and it finally happened after 323 minutes and 54 seconds of play in 2012.

"I told to them at halftime, 'Listen, what did you think, we were going to go the whole year and not trail and do that the whole year?'" Kelly said. "You don't do that in college football, at any level.' I said, 'Stick with the plan.'"

The victory, ND's sixth without a lost

Notre Dame senior tight end Tyler Eifert wins a jump ball with Stanford's Devon Carrington (left) and Terrance Brown, pulling in a touchdown pass to tie the game 10-10. The Irish held on for a physical 20-13 win over the Cardinal. South Bend Tribune/ROBERT FRANKLIN

his season and one that inches the Irish closer to the center of the national championship conversation, was decorated with the usual gaudy defensive landmarks.

The Irish continue to be the stingiest ND incarnation in scoring defense since 1976 with 49 points through six games. Dan Devine's '76 team yielded 43 through six. ND's last two national titlists gave up 78 (1977) and 91 (1988), respectively, over the same span.

The ND defense extended their streak to 16 quarters without an offensive touchdown. Stanford's lone trip into the Irish end zone came on one of Golson's three lost fumbles, this one when Stanford defensive end Ben Gardner separated Golson from the ball in the end zone and linebacker Chase Thomas pounced on it.

That gave the Cardinal a 7-3 lead with 6:06 left in the second quarter. The Irish didn't retake the lead until the overtime period, when relief quarterback Tommy Rees wiggled out of a second-and-18 situation with a 10-yard pass to DaVaris Daniels, a 16-yard sideline pass to Theo Riddick while facing a blitz and the game-winning seven-yarder to TJ Jones in succession.

Rees entered the game with 3:24 left in regulation and the Irish driving but down 13-10. That came just after Golson took a helmet to his head while scrambling, a hit that drew a 15-yard penalty on Stanford.

"Blow to the head and his vision was blurred," Kelly said. "He wanted to get back in, and our medical personnel would not clear him."

Eight plays later, sophomore Kyle Brindza tied the game at 13-13 with a 22-yard field goal with 23 seconds left in regulation.

The defense eventually made it stand up.

The Irish, the lone team in the 120-team BCS not to have given up a rushing touchdown this season, protracted that streak to 34 quarters, dating back to last year's BC game.

Stanford (4-2) came as close as anyone, pounding the ball up the gut four straight times in overtime after gaining a first and goal at the Irish 4-yard line and trailing 20-13.

Notre Dame cornerback Bennett Jackson—a converted wide receiver—kills a Stanford drive by picking off a Josh Nunes pass intended for Brian Gottfried. The Irish defense repeatedly stepped up big in the overtime win. South Bend Tribune/JAMES BROSHER

Senior running back Stepfan Taylor, the nation's 15th-leading rusher, pounded one yard on first down, two and some change on second, then got stood up for no gain on third, leading to both the most telling and most dramatic play of the season.

"No matter what happens, everybody stood together," Irish senior linebacker Manti Te'o, the central figure in ND's resurgence, told his teammates just before the final play.

Had Stanford quarterback Josh Nunes faked the handoff to Taylor on fourth down and made a move to the outside, he might have been able to walk in. But it never entered Cardinal coach David Shaw's mind.

"That," he said about power, in-your-face football, "is what we do."

And throwing a season-changing counterpunch to the football bully, that had pushed the Irish around on both sides of the line of scrimmage for the past two meetings especially, is what the Irish did.

Linebacker Carlo Calabrese, who started the year on the suspended list, and cornerback Bennett Jackson, a former wide receiver who began the season as a question mark, surged at Taylor as he tried to contort into the end zone.

"There's no question," Kelly responded with a big smile when asked if the way the Irish won—muscle and will against muscle and will—was as satisfying as the win itself. "Look, when you're talking to your team all week about a heavyweight match, you can't keep taking body blows. You have to stand in there, and sooner or later, you've got to be the one that delivers. Classic."

The Irish lost the turnover battle for the first time this season, 3-2, but Jackson and free safety Matthias Farley each had interceptions in Irish territory to thwart Stanford scoring drives.

"We have a lot of room for improvement," Irish nose guard Louis Nix said. "We gave up three points (on defense), and that's three too many. We just want to keep working to be the best defense in the country. We've got a long way to go." ■

Irish players and the Notre Dame band react after the Irish defense stopped Stanford on 4th-and-1 in overtime to seal the victory over Stanford. South Bend Tribune/ROBERT FRANKLIN

5

INSIDE LINEBACKER

MANTI TE'O

What dreams may come

By Eric Hansen • October 12, 2012

It never felt like a chance meeting, although it probably appeared that way from the outside looking in. Their stares got pleasantly tangled, then Manti Te'o extended his hand to the stranger with a warm smile and soulful eyes.

They could have just as easily brushed past each other and into separate sunsets. Te'o had plenty to preoccupy himself that November weekend in Palo Alto, Calif., back in 2009.

His Notre Dame football team hadn't won since Halloween, and a three-game losing streak that included seismic home setbacks to Navy and Connecticut, was pushing Irish head coach Charlie Weis out the door after five seasons, albeit with a seven-figure financial settlement set to kick in.

Weis was the man who, in the recruiting process, promised Te'o's parents that he would take care of their son 4,400 miles away, that he would make sure he graduated and really nothing else, nothing that had anything to do with football anyway.

And once Te'o's 11th-hour shift away from USC and to Notre Dame took hold, Te'o's still-confusing leap of faith hinged upon every subsequent word that came from Weis.

The part that stung the most for the Laie, Hawaii,

product was that there was nothing he could do in ND's upcoming clash with Stanford that could reverse the process. His only anchor was about to be set adrift.

There had been delusions by some observers, going into the '09 season, that the freshman linebacker would be so advanced, so transformational, so immune to growing pains and flat spots in the growth curve that he could help launch the Irish back into a cycle of national prominence.

Instead, it was a school with an even smaller recruiting pool and a less-decorated football tradition that prevailed, 45-38, in what turned out to be Weis' last game. That same school, Stanford, then proceeded to smack around the old stereotype of needing to compromise academic standards in order to climb up on college football's biggest postseason stages.

Te'o would start the game on the bench and finish it with a new career high in tackles, with 10.

This Saturday afternoon at Notre Dame Stadium, three years later and half a continent away, Stanford and the Irish meet again, this time with Notre Dame ascending and Te'o right in the middle of the uprising.

The Cardinal (4-1), ranked 17th, have won three

Manti Te'o salutes the crowd after his second interception of the game during Notre Dame's Sept. 22 win over Michigan. Fans wearing leis filled the stands that night in support of the Hawaiian-born Irish linebacker, who lost his grandmother and girlfriend earlier in the month. South Bend Tribune/ROBERT FRANKLIN

straight in the series and have pushed around the Irish in the process. ND (5-0), which started the season unranked, has pushed itself into the cusp of the national title conversation.

For the first time this season and seventh time in Te'o's career, his parents, Brian and Ottilia, will be in the stands for the game—along with the youngest of his five siblings, 6-year-old brother Manasseh.

"They're watching you and they're watching someone who they've given everything they have to live his dream," Te'o said earlier this week. "My dream is to help them in their dream, too. So, it's always exciting. It's going to be a special occasion to see them in the stands."

And Manti Te'o is convinced the beautiful stranger will be watching, too, Saturday, somehow.

Lennay Kekua was a Stanford student and Cardinal football fan when the two exchanged glances, handshakes and phone numbers that fateful weekend three seasons ago.

She was gifted in music, multilingual, had dreams grounded in reality and the talent to catch up to them.

The plan was for Kekua to spend extensive time with the whole Te'o family when upwards of 40 of them came to South Bend in mid-November for ND's Senior Day date with Wake Forest.

"They started out as just friends," Brian Te'o said. "Every once in a while, she would travel to Hawaii, and that happened to be the time Manti was home, so he would meet with her there. But within the last year, they became a couple.

"And we came to the realization that she could be our daughter-in-law. Sadly, it won't happen now."

About the time Kekua and Manti became a couple, she was injured in an auto accident. There were complications during her recovery. And it was also during her recovery that it was discovered Kekua had leukemia.

"That was just in June," Brian Te'o said. "I remember Manti telling me later she was going to have a bone marrow transplant and, sure enough, that's exactly what happened. From all I knew, she was doing really, really well."

Kekua, who eventually graduated from Stanford, was, in fact, doing so well that she was released from the hospital on Sept. 10. And Brian Te'o was among those congratulating her via telephone.

Less than 48 hours later, at 4 a.m. Hawaii time, Kekua sent a text to Brian and Ottilia, expressing her condolences over the passing of Ottilia's mom, Annette Santiago, just hours before.

Brian awakened three hours later, saw the text, and sent one back. There was no response. A couple of hours later, Manti called his parents, his heart in pieces.

Lennay Kekua had died.

In a Newport Beach, Calif., hotel room last December, Brian Te'o pulled out the papers with the numbers Manti had asked him to compile, figuring it was only a formality in what seemed like an obvious decision to go pro a year early.

Manti and his parents had all flown to California for a banquet honoring the Lott Impact Award finalists, but at the top of the agenda was putting the finer points on how to break the news to ND head coach Brian Kelly and the rest of the college football world that Te'o's junior year at the school would indeed be his last.

Instead, it was Manti who had to break the news. In the days leading up to this moment, BrieAnne Te'o was among the voices whose words pervaded in Manti's thoughts.

The oldest of Manti's four sisters asked him point blank over the phone, "Wasn't it your dream to go to the NFL? Then go."

But as the words fermented and mixed with Manti's prayers, he came to what sounded like a chance decision, at least from the outside looking in.

"The NFL is my goal, not my dream," he told his parents. "My dream is to have an impact on people. I think I'm doing that, and I'm not finished yet."

Brian's and Ottilia's pride overran their tear ducts as the surprising decision sunk in.

"I never said it to Manti, but I did wonder, 'Man, what more can you do?'" Brian said. "And then on Sept. 22, I knew. We all knew."

That was the night of ND's clash with Michigan, the first home game after Santiago and Kekua had passed. In fact, Kekua's funeral was held in California earlier that morning.

Brian and Ottilia were back in Laie, watching the game on TV, and overwhelmed with emotion before the opening kickoff.

"They kind of panned out and took a wide view of the stadium," Brian said, "and all you could see from corner to corner on my television were these leis. They were twirling on people's fingers and I turned to my wife and I said, 'That's for your son.'"

Seemingly, the entire student section was adorned in them, band members, cheerleaders—even the people who typically implore the ushers to ask people to sit down and shut up. On the couple's Facebook page, people took pictures of their kids in Manti's No. 5 jersey, wearing leis.

"From Texas, from California, from Utah, from London," Ottilia said.

"One guy had his children making a No. 5 with their bodies, laying down on the lawn with their leis on," Brian said. "I even got a picture from a Michigan fan. He was wearing his Michigan jersey, but he had a lei on. He said, 'I love Michigan, but I support your son.'

"And I go back to that night at the Lott Awards. I should have known. It shouldn't have been a surprise to me that his intention was to just unite as many people under a single idea of family. I didn't think it would get to this level."

But Brian never doubted that Manti would choose to play through the tragedy in both the Michigan game and the road game at Michigan State that preceded it.

"He said something that night in Newport Beach that kind of scared me, actually," Brian said. "He said 'Dad, whether I'm on crutches or in pads, I'm going to run out of the tunnel my last game, and it's then I'm going to be able to say to Notre Dame, I gave you everything. Wherever we land, that's where we'll be.'"

In the moments after the Michigan game, Ottilia sent Manti a text with a familiar message, "Thanks for choosing me as your mom."

"Our belief, as members of the church, is that before we came here to this Earth, that we got to choose our circumstance in life," Ottilia said. "And I'm just so grateful, as a parent, that when Manti was up there he chose Brian and I—he chose us to be his parents. Definitely we had a lot of work to do. He was literally with us every step of the way."

Brian and Ottilia were 19 when they got married, and Manti came along shortly thereafter.

"We were young parents," Brian said, "and there was something about that kid that brought a sense of peace and order to what ordinarily would be a very chaotic young relationship.

"We went from teenagers to parents almost overnight. I told my wife that this kid is special. 'There's something about him that makes the world better.'

"When he was 2 or 3 we tried to explain to him, 'There's something special that you're supposed to do. We don't know what it is, but we're going to do everything we can do to help you find it.'"

Even if that sometimes meant letting him make his most profound decisions on his own—to attend Notre Dame, not to take a two-year Mormon Mission weeks after Kelly succeeded Weis, to return for his senior year and to play through the grief and the pain.

All seemed rather disconnected at the time, but almost seem steeped in destiny now.

"We listen to his interviews on the Internet pretty regularly, and we kept hearing him talk recently about him making our dreams come true," Ottilia said. "I think, in his mind, he's thinking huge house, I can tell. But that's not what our dreams look like."

What they look like is the conversation between Kelly and Manti that Brian Te'o overheard on Skype just after the double tragedies hit him. "I was so worried about him," Brian said, "but what coach Kelly said made me know he was with family."

What they look like is Manti Te'o doing what he promised in that Newport Beach hotel room, making a difference every day.

"As my wife suggested, our dream is to watch our children live theirs," Brian said. "And right now I'd say we're right in the middle of that." ∎

OCTOBER 20, 2012 • SOUTH BEND, INDIANA
NOTRE DAME 17, BYU 14

Performance So-So, But 7-0

ND wobbles, but run game, defense delivers

By Eric Hansen

In the muted celebration, Cierre Wood stood defiant, convinced that the statistical carnage wreaked on the nation's third-ranked rushing defense wasn't an anomaly, but the start of something.

"There's not anybody on our schedule or in the country who we don't think we can run the ball against," the Notre Dame senior running back said after the fifth-ranked Irish cobbled together a 17-14 comeback victory over BYU Saturday at Notre Dame Stadium. "I don't care if they were first (in rushing defense), we're going to run the ball. That's exactly what we did."

Actually, the Irish gouged the BYU defense for 270 rushing yards after it had never given up more than 110 in a game this season, frittered all but 20 seconds of the final 6:10 following an Irish defensive stand, averaged 6.3 yards a carry against a unit whose average yield was 2.2 and did it without even the hint of the element of surprise.

Wood had 114 of those yards on 18 carries. Fellow senior Theo Riddick rushed for a career-high 143 on 15 carries, including a 55-yarder in which he kept his balance when it looked like he would be stopped at the line of scrimmage.

This Irish attempted just three passes in the second half (and 17 for the game) as they moved to 7-0 for the 25th time in school history but the first since the offensively challenged 2002 Tyrone Willingham-coached squad ran off eight wins to start the season.

All this from a rushing offense that stood 80th nationally out of 120 FBS teams entering the month of October, struggled early in the season to knit a new zone-blocking scheme into an offense that featured rotating quarterbacks and green receivers.

BYU linebacker Kyle Van Noy breaks up a pass intended for Notre Dame's TJ Jones. Playing without starting quarterback Everett Golson, the Irish completed only eight of 17 pass attempts. South Bend Tribune/ROBERT FRANKLIN

For the record, junior Tommy Rees made his 18th career start, with minimal relief from third-stringer Andrew Hendrix, after Kelly decided to err on the side of caution with No. 1 quarterback Everett Golson. Golson suffered a concussion late in the fourth quarter of last Saturday's 20-13 overtime win over Stanford, and Kelly decided Friday after a team walk-through to take him out of play.

"He wanted to play," Kelly said of the sophomore, first-year starter. "He made his case. I just felt like this was the best thing to do.

"He was supportive. He was great on the sideline. But he clearly—he wanted to get in there as well. We feel like we've got a kid now that's 100 percent ready to go for Oklahoma."

Even with Golson having to shake the cobwebs next Saturday for the biggest road start of his fledgling career, Kelly feels at least another missing piece in an offense with still plenty of room to grow fell into place against the Cougars.

The running game.

"We are becoming that kind of football team on offense," Kelly said. "You talk about finding an identity. Even when we were down, we kept running the football."

And ND did get down early, falling behind 14-7 midway through the first half on a pair of touchdown passes from rugged BYU senior quarterback Riley Nelson, who was a freshman at Utah State in 2006 the last time Notre Dame was on a BCS trajectory this late in the season.

The first came with 8:25 left in the second quarter, when BYU leading receiver Cody Hoffman got loose in the back of the end zone for a six-yard strike on third down. That broke a string of 17 consecutive quarters by the Irish defense without allowing a touchdown.

The second Cougars score followed a Rees interception that glanced off Irish sophomore DaVaris Daniels' hands and into the arms of BYU linebacker Kyle Van Noy.

The 30-yard drive ended with a Nelson two-yard pass to tight end Kaneakua Friel for a 14-7 BYU lead. Sopho-more kicker Kyle Brindza missed a pair of first-half field goals for the Irish, including a 28-yarder 2:30 before halftime.

The Irish closed to within 14-10 on a Brindza 24-yard field goal with 2:55 left in the third quarter and surged ahead on a George Atkinson III four-yard run on the next Irish possession. Rees' only completion of the second half, a 31-yard strike to TJ Jones after a 6-for-7 start, was followed by running, running and more running.

BYU then took possession on its own 16 after the kickoff with 12:48 left and held the ball for more than six minutes. But the Cougars faced a fourth-and-13 from the Irish 34 and decided to punt.

"We really believed we would stop them and get the ball back with better field position than what we did," BYU coach Bronco Mendenhall said.

BYU did get the ball back, but at its own 20 with no timeouts left and 22 seconds left. Danny Spond picked off Nelson with two ticks remaining, and the Irish took a knee to finish a part-convincing, part-wobbly victory.

The Irish defense did its part after the jolting start. The Irish held the Cougars to 66 rushing yards and 243 total yards in the game. It's the sixth straight game ND's opponent hasn't reached the 300-yard mark in total offense—the longest such streak since the 1983 Irish put together eight straight such games.

Irish senior linebacker Manti Te'o again led the way with 10 tackles and his fourth interception of the season. He's now one off the single-season school record for picks by a linebacker, shared by Lyron Cobbins (1995) and John Pergine (1966).

"It goes back to the saying, 'Defense wins championships,'" Te'o said. "When we get into these close games, the mentality now is we are going to do whatever it takes to win. It's no longer we're crossing our fingers and going 'please, please, please,' waiting for the next shoe to drop.

"We are all just trying to be that person who makes things happen." ∎

Notre Dame defenders (from left) Manti Te'o, Louis Nix III, and Stephon Tuitt take down BYU running back Jamaal Williams. The Irish defense limited the Cougars to 66 yards on the ground. South Bend Tribune/JAMES BROSHER

OCTOBER 27, 2012 • NORMAN, OKLAHOMA
NOTRE DAME 30, OKLAHOMA 13

ND To Doubters: Take That!

Exceptional effort sacks Oklahoma

By Eric Hansen

This was the week when Notre Dame's surreality was supposed to dead end into college football's next wave of reality.

Fast-tempo, overwhelming, pass-happy offense, the kind that Irish head coach Brian Kelly has actually morphed away from.

The national come-uppance in the clash of cultures never materialized. Only a seismic affirmation that fifth-ranked Notre Dame is taking its improbable national title dreams into November and perhaps beyond.

Irish middle linebacker Manti Te'o provided the knockout blow in a 30-13 ND uprising over No. 8 Oklahoma, a 12-point favorite coming into the clash between the two teams that have spent the most time in history at the top of the AP poll.

The ever-building Heisman Trophy contender's fifth interception of the season with 4:27 left set up Kyle Brindza's

game-clinching field goal 65 seconds later, in a surge of smashmouth dominance and just enough finesse to give the human voters and computers that comprise the BCS' mathematics something to think about.

Irish running back Theo Riddick pounded in from 15 yards out to provide the exclamation point for only the second non-conference home loss in Sooners' coach Bob Stoops' 14 seasons in Oklahoma. It was just the fifth home loss overall in the 84 games in which Stoops has been stalking the Sooner sidelines in Norman.

ND (8-0) then added the defensive equivalent of style points in the closing seconds after Oklahoma (5-2) had reached the 1-yard line. The Sooners then backpedaled, with the game ending on a Prince Shembo sack of Oklahoma quarterback Landry Jones.

"Notre Dame made the key plays down

Quarterback Everett Golson looks to pass during Notre Dame's 30-13 win over Oklahoma. In his breakout performance, the first-year starter completed 13 of 25 passes—including a 50-yard heave to freshman Chris Brown to set up the go-ahead touchdown in the fourth quarter. South Bend Tribune/JAMES BROSHER

the stretch when they needed them," Stoops said.

Oklahoma had pulled even at 13-13 with 9:10 left in the game and broke Notre Dame's nation's longest active streak of not allowing a rushing touchdown when Oklahoma's 6-foot-6, 256-pound battering ram of a situational quarterback, Blake Bell, battered in from one yard out. It was Bell's 22nd rushing touchdown in 14 games and truncated the Irish streak without a rushing TD at 41 quarters going back to Senior Day against Boston College in game 11 of last season.

It was a Bell pass, though—just the 17th of his career—that was the key play on the drive. He connected with fullback Trey Millard on an eight-yard pass play just prior to his TD plunge on fourth-and-2 from the Irish nine.

From there, Notre Dame answered. And answered. And answered again.

Irish quarterback Everett Golson, who sat out last week's BYU escape while recovering from a concussion, engineered the most impressive drive of his seven-game career—73 yards in seven plays.

"I thought Everett Golson led our team," Kelly said. "He had been challenged to continue to grow. It's been a process, but I thought tonight was a big step up for our quarterback and our offense elevated itself against great competition on the road."

Golson finished 13-of-25 passing for 177 yards, rushed 11 times for 64 yards and played turnover-free.

Freshman Chris Brown's first career reception, a 50-yarder, set up a head-first dive by Golson five plays later for the go-ahead score. That left Oklahoma 5:05 with which to volley.

But on a first-down pass from Oklahoma's 41, Jones threw to Fresno State transfer Jalen Saunders, who had gouged ND's defense all night, but Irish linebacker Dan Fox jarred Saunders and the ball careened into the air and eventually into the arms of a diving Te'o for an interception.

Saunders finished with 15 catches for 185 yards in just his third game in an Oklahoma uniform. But the difference came in the run game.

Running back Cierre Wood breaks away from the Oklahoma defense and rushes 62 yards into the end zone to give the Irish a 7-3 first-quarter lead. South Bend Tribune/JAMES BROSHER

A record Memorial Stadium crowd of 86,031 looked on as the Irish dominated the line of scrimmage on both sides of the ball, outrushing Oklahoma 215-15. Notre Dame was coming off its most prolific three-game rushing burst (796 yards) in nine years.

The 10th meeting ever and first under the lights and first in Norman since ND's 1966 national championship run saw Oklahoma score first on a 28-yard field goal by Michael Hunnicutt at the 7:12 mark of the first quarter.

The Irish responded with a 62-yard TD run up the middle from Cierre Wood, the longest offensive play of the season for ND and the longest run of the senior running back's career.

The Irish and Sooners then traded field goals as Notre Dame took a 10-6 lead at the half.

But Notre Dame surged in the third quarter and overwhelmed in the fourth. ■

Left: Everett Golson contributed with his legs as well as his arm. The quarterback rushed for 64 yards on 11 carries, including a 1-yard run to put the Irish ahead in the fourth quarter. Above: Cornerback Bennett Jackson celebrates with fans following Notre Dame's win in Norman, Oklahoma. South Bend Tribune/JAMES BROSHER

6
RUNNING BACK
THEO RIDDICK
No maybes about Irish back
By Al Lesar • December 3, 2012

There has to be a reason—tangible or intangible—why Theo Riddick played like he did for Notre Dame this season.

Maybe it was the internal sense of urgency a football player finds in his senior year.

Maybe it was physical maturity.

Maybe it was emotional maturity.

Maybe it was him finally getting a thorough understanding of expectations.

Maybe it was the coaching staff finally getting a thorough understanding of him.

Maybe it was a total commitment to a goal that had never been made before.

The 5-foot-11, 200-pound running back didn't even vaguely resemble the Theo Riddick who struggled to find his niche—whether it was in the backfield or as a receiver—in his first three years in the Irish program.

This guy ran with a purpose. On 174 carries, Riddick had just 24 negative yards. Riddick is a missile when he approaches the point of contact. A play that's stuffed can go for five yards in a hurry.

That's a big difference for the Irish offense. That sort of production—860 rushing yards and five TDs—made a profound impact on this season. Add in 32 pass receptions for 306 yards and a touchdown, and the hybrid running back/slot receiver has finally found his niche.

"We wanted to bring a more physical presence to our football team," Riddick said. "I think I exemplified that, along with others. What can I say? Things just worked out well this year. I really don't have the answer (why)."

It might be too simple to suggest that just having more opportunities led to the success. Opportunities came because of the production. A chicken and the egg scenario.

"I guess you could say I was in the backfield more; I got more touches," said Riddick, who had played mostly receiver during his sophomore and junior years. "We have a great offensive coordinator (Chuck Martin) and offensive line. Everything worked out well this year."

Irish senior running back Theo Riddick jukes Trojans linebacker Tony Burnett following in a reception in Notre Dame's Nov. 24 win over USC. Riddick—who played both receiver and running back during his career—totaled 146 yards on the ground and 33 in the air against USC. South Bend Tribune/JAMES BROSHER

It's easy to compare Riddick to what running back Jonas Gray accomplished last year. Gray was another guy who floundered through his first three seasons, then made his mark (791 rushing yards, 12 TDs) as a senior.

That final push, despite a knee injury late in the season, earned Gray an NFL roster spot this season. Odds are it could do the same for Riddick.

That's down the road, though. All that's on his mind now is turning that underdog role into a national championship.

"We've been going through (being an underdog) this whole season, in terms of gaining respect," Riddick said. "You can't get all tied up into that. All we can do is control what we can control and do the best we can in this national championship game."

That control starts with more than a month's worth of study and preparation to know the Crimson Tide inside and out.

"This will help us in knowing Alabama," Riddick said of the next 30 days or so. "They're the defending champs. You want to beat the best. We have that chance."

Besides production, limiting mistakes is another key for Irish success. Last year, Notre Dame lost 12 fumbles. This year, they've yielded seven. On his 174 carries, Riddick has lost just one fumble—against Boston College.

"With that great of a team (as Alabama), or any team, actually, you turn the ball over and you lessen your chances to win," Riddick said.

At this point, with this challenge, there's no room to lessen the chances.

Give the ball to Riddick.

No maybes about it. ■

Theo Riddick breaks away during Notre Dame's win over BYU on Oct. 20 at Notre Dame Stadium. Riddick rushed for 143 yards on 15 carries. South Bend Tribune/ROBERT FRANKLIN

NOVEMBER 3, 2012 • SOUTH BEND, INDIANA

NOTRE DAME 29, PITT 26

Irish Survive, Learn Lesson

ND fends off unranked Pitt in 3 overtimes

By Eric Hansen

What the celebration lacked in its unevenness, it made up for in awkwardness.

The Notre Dame student section spilled onto the field in bits and pieces, running toward the hero of the third overtime, quarterback Everett Golson, almost more out of relief than reveling over where the 29-26 marathon survival of unranked, uncelebrated and undaunted Pittsburgh on Saturday might take the fourth-ranked Irish.

"Last year this would have been a loss," Notre Dame third-year head coach Brian Kelly insisted.

For most of the 60 minutes of regulation and three overtime periods at Notre Dame Stadium, it could have been something much more devastating.

The pulse temporarily stopped on both ND's dark horse national title hopes and linebacker Manti Te'o's unorthodox Heisman Trophy chase. But Pitt's level of scoreboard shock was so thorough early in the fourth quarter and so unexpected, the Irish could have slipped out of a certain BCS trajectory and into bowl limbo if they did anything less than sweep Boston College, Wake Forest and USC the next three weeks.

Instead Notre Dame heads to arch-rival BC, 9-0 for the 16th time in school history but for the first time since the year Golson was born (1993). That after trailing 20-6 in the fourth quarter, losing the turnover battle 3-0, taking a quantum leap backward on special teams, and having running back Cierre Wood fumble at the goal line in the second overtime.

"Today was a wakeup call to really focus on us," said Te'o, somewhat of a peripheral figure in the game until the Irish defense surged in the fourth quarter and the over-

Pitt cornerback K'Waun Williams hits ND quarterback Everett Golson as Golson releases the ball during the first quarter. The first-year starter struggled early and was replaced by Tommy Rees in the fourth quarter, before leading Notre Dame's comeback in the fourth quarter and overtime. South Bend Tribune/JAMES BROSHER

time sessions. He finished with seven tackles, six of which came after Pitt (5-4) took a 10-6 halftime lead, as well as a half sack and a pass deflection.

And the Irish did wake up in time to score only the second comeback in the past nine years in which they trailed by 11 or more points. A Brady Quinn-led rally over Michigan State in 2006 was the other. The Irish trailed in that one, 37-21, before rallying for the 40-37 triumph.

At the end of the day Saturday, the Irish looked statistically like the 17-point favorite the odds-makers set that at. ND tied a school record with 34 first downs, to Pitt's 13. They also held commanding advantages in offensive plays (a school-record 104 to 62), total yards (522-308) and time of possession (35:23-24:37). And they held the Panthers to one third-down conversion in 14 tries.

But they strayed from the team that played with an edge and precision through most of its first eight games and in particular its 30-13 smackdown of Oklahoma last weekend in Norman, Okla. Their swagger waned, and Kelly's offensive play-calling at times reeked of a man bent on style points.

He even took the relief quarterback concept to a new extreme. But when it mattered most, the Irish found themselves, the defense rose to vintage form and Golson was smack in the middle of the late offensive pyrotechnics.

Golson finished 23-of-42 for 227 yards and two TDs. A total of 105 yards of those came in the fourth quarter and overtime sessions. He also ran for 59 yards on nine carries, including a TD and two-point conversion after the third quarter, that after amassing 15 yards on six carries through the first six periods.

"I thought he competed his butt off," Kelly said. "He's not perfect, but the boy competes. And, man, he just kept competing in the second half and found a way for us to get enough points on the board, so he got the game ball."

Golson's one-yard dive into the end zone over center Braxston Cave in the third OT answered Kevin Harper's 44-yard field goal for Pitt earlier in the third extra session and capped the most roller-coaster day of Golson's already

Panthers cornerback K'Waun Williams intercepts a pass intended for Irish tight end Troy Niklas in the end zone. The turnover gave Pitt an eight-point lead and the ball with less than four minutes remaining in the game. South Bend Tribune/ROBERT FRANKLIN

81

up-and-down existence as Notre Dame's No, 1 quarterback.

He was benched briefly, but was reinstated after a Tommy Rees interception in the third quarter. The sophomore responded with two fourth-quarter scoring drives sandwiched around his own pick in the end zone with 3:59 left in regulation and the Irish still trailing by eight.

"I get a sense of feel on the sideline as to where to move with that," Kelly said of his decision to start Rees in the second half. "I went up to (Golson) when I thought we needed him back in the game, because of the way the game was going. Our quarterback needed to be out there mobile, make some plays outside the pocket. I asked him if he was ready to go. He said he was, and we put him back in."

Golson's first touchdown pass went to TJ Jones, an 11-yarder on what was a bit of a misdirection play. Kicker Kyle Brindza missed the extra point off a high snap and the deficit was 20-12 at the 13:40 mark of the fourth quarter.

After Pitt cornerback K'waun Williams seemingly sealed the upset with an interception of a short Golson pass intended for tight end Troy Niklas, the Irish defense forced a three-and-out.

The Irish took possession on the 50 with 3:03 left. On the first play, Golson extended the play with his feet, found DaVaris Daniels streaking down field and threw a bit of a jumpball to him for a 45-yard gain.

The next play, Golson fired a five-yard strike to Theo Riddick on an out route that landed the Irish running back in the ND marching band after the score. Golson added the two-point conversion, rolling to his left, then knifing through the defense and diving into the end zone when his two receiving options were well-covered.

"For me it's all God and my teammates," Golson said. "Robby Toma came up and said keep your head in the game. A whole bunch of guys did that, I came out a little flat. I missed some reads, but in the stretch we really came together. I'm just happy that my teammates trusted me and believed in me."

After both teams labored to move the ball in the final two minutes of regulation, Pitt and Notre Dame traded field goals in the first OT—a 41-yarder from Harper and a 37-yarder from Brindza.

Then it got weird. The Irish pounded the ball with their running game in the second OT. The Irish had a second-and goal from the 2, when Wood went airborne but lost the ball just before he broke the plane of the goal line. Pitt safety Jarred Holley recovered.

All Pitt had to do was kick the game-winning field goal. And after running Ray Graham three times in a row, the Panthers settled for a 33-yarder on fourth and 1. Harper pushed it right, and the teams moved to the third overtime.

That's where the Irish relocated their national title dream, however faint and unlikely. At least it still existed.

"Our coaches stayed positive," Kelly said, "and were there for our players when things weren't going well. It was not, 'It's your fault. This is why we're not winning.' It was, 'Get back to what you do and how you do it.' I was just really proud of my staff and the way they executed the game plan and stuck with it."

"Next week BC will play out of their minds against us, and Wake Forest will. And they (the Irish players) can't just highlight certain teams on their schedule, because they will play their very best. I think that's a lesson learned for our football team." ▪

Irish running back Cierre Wood pauses for a moment during the celebration following Notre Dame's 29-26 overtime win over Pitt. Students rushed the field after Everett Golson scored a touchdown to complete the comeback victory. South Bend Tribune/ROBERT FRANKLIN

NOVEMBER 10, 2012 · CHESTNUT HILL, MASSACHUSETTS
NOTRE DAME 21, BOSTON COLLEGE 6

Irish Steady, Not Stylish

Victory over BC has share of flaws

By Eric Hansen

Amidst the intermittent sloppiness, the lack of offensive pyrotechnics and a storyline that never ventured into something worthy of a prime-time time slot, almost unnoticed it happened.

Notre Dame head football coach Brian Kelly finally euthanized the tag-team quarterback concept, tossed away the training wheels and watched sophomore QB Everett Golson flourish as a full-time starter and closer in an otherwise unaesthetic 21-6 conquest of historical nemesis Boston College.

Golson didn't wow with record-breaking numbers, but rather command, efficiency, guile and play-making. The fourth-ranked Irish converted their first 10 third downs of the game, played keepaway with their running game and got enough glue from Golson to run their record to 10-0 for the eighth time in school history and the first since 1993.

That also happens to be the last season ND was this serious of a national title threat this late in the season.

That status late Saturday night had more to do with top-ranked Alabama's upset loss at home to Texas A&M than anything that could have been construed as style points against a 2-8 Boston College team likely two games away from a head coaching search.

"We did a nice job on third down," Kelly said. "I think our quarterback play was really good. One of the best plays I think he's had is when he put his foot in the ground, ran north to south. We were effective tonight because our quarterback play was effective tonight."

The Irish defense, underwhelming at times, did finish with a surge of dominance, with linebacker Manti Te'o capping a relatively quiet night with an interception to kill

Irish linebacker Manti Te'o pulled down his sixth interception of the season in the fourth quarter. South Bend Tribune/ROBERT FRANKLIN

one late BC drive, Kapron Lewis-Moore killing another with a fourth-down sack of BC quarterback Chase Rettig and Prince Shembo adding a fumble recovery to his game-high three sacks.

For Te'o, it was his sixth pick of the season, giving him the single-season school record for interceptions by a linebacker. And Shembo's three sacks are the most by an Irish player since Victor Abiamiri recorded three versus Stanford six seasons ago. Abiamiri was also the last Irish player to record four—also against Stanford, in 2005.

Overall, the Irish have allowed 111 points this season. Only coach Dan Devine's 1980 team yielded fewer among ND defenses since coaching legend Ara Parseghian walked away from the profession following the 1974 season.

"I thought our kids understood that they have to play really hard," said Kelly, now 8-3 on the road at ND and 11-5 in night games in his three years with the Irish with a five-game winning streak under the lights. "The only thing I'm not happy with is the turnovers. They played hard and physical for four quarters."

George Atkinson and Cierre Wood each lost fumbles. That's three total since the second overtime of last weekend's triple-overtime survival of Pitt. Up until Wood coughed it up at the goal line in that game, the Irish running backs had gone 277 carries without a lost fumble.

Golson finished 16-of-24 for 200 yards with two TD passes and zero interceptions. He also ran for 39 yards on 11 carries and his fifth rushing touchdown of the season— the most by an Irish QB since Jarious Jackson notched seven in 1999. The Irish converted on all of their red-zone chances against the Eagles.

The somber note on the night was that sophomore wide receiver DaVaris Daniels left the game with an apparent shoulder injury. His father, former NFL defensive end Phillip Daniels, intimated via his Twitter account Saturday night that the injury appears to be of the long-term variety.

Kelly acknowledged an MRI would be taken.

But Notre Dame still needs more help if it's going to land in the national championship game Jan. 7 in Miami.

"We're going to work on winning against Wake Forest," Kelly said. "When it's all said and done, we'll see where we are. We really can't waste any of our energy on worrying about those things." ∎

Left: Notre Dame freshman Romeo Okwara (45) celebrates after tackling Boston College's Spiffy Evans on a kick return late in the second quarter. Above: Safety Zeke Motta sticks out his tongue as the Irish walk off the field following Notre Dame's 10th win of the season. South Bend Tribune/ROBERT FRANKLIN

80
TIGHT END
TYLER EIFERT
From decoy to dominant
By Al Lesar • November 20, 2012

Statistics never seemed much of a priority for Tyler Eifert; at least the public Tyler Eifert, whom Notre Dame football fans have come to know.

The 6-foot-6, 251-pound senior tight end didn't wince once during a three-game stretch—Michigan State through Miami—in which he caught just three passes.

"As long as the team's winning...," was his mantra. "If we weren't winning, that would be different."

Fair enough. Sad to see a pair of soft hands attached to a quite athletic body wasted as a blocker and a decoy, though.

He never squawked. But, that's just who Eifert is. He never tried to be the furry face of the Irish program. He never tried to lobby the emotional heart and soul of the team away from Manti Te'o.

Eifert, a John Mackey Award finalist, just did his job.

The game plan started to find him again. In wins over Pitt, Boston College and Wake Forest he caught 18 passes for 214 yards and a touchdown. His fifth reception against the Demon Deacons, in the third quarter, was the 129th of his career, making Eifert the most prolific pass-catching tight end in Notre

Dame history. He passed Ken MacAfee (1974-77), a member the College Football Hall of Fame.

What seemed out of place was Eifert's post-game reaction to eclipsing the reception record. Rather than taking the milestone in stride, he sounded more like Roger Maris after he finally passed Babe Ruth's single-season home run mark in the '60s—like he was somewhat of a reluctant participant in a competition that had gone far beyond his scope.

"I was real happy to have (the record)," Eifert said. "I was happy that I don't have to think about it anymore. You could say what you want, say you're 'not thinking about it,' but you know right where you are (in relation to MacAfee).

"Coach (Brian) Kelly said, 'If you drop this, we're not throwing to you the rest of the game.' I made sure I caught it."

Maybe there's more going on in Eifert's mind than he lets on.

Remember, this was a guy whose playing career at Notre Dame nearly ended before it started. Some serious back issues not only kept him off the field as a freshman, but made medical folks wonder if his body would hold up.

Tyler Eifert makes a move after hauling in one of his four catches against Purdue on Sept. 8. The tight end led the Irish with 98 receiving yards. South Bend Tribune/JAMES BROSHER

"I'm just thankful for a long and healthy career that put me in a position to get the record," said Eifert, not taking anything for granted. "It doesn't feel like it was too long ago (when his career was in question). There was definitely a real thought that I wouldn't (be able to play). That wasn't the case and I'm grateful for that."

So are the Irish. Eleven wins into the season, he and TJ Jones are tied for the team lead in receptions with 40. Eifert has collected 555 yards, 36 more than Jones. He and Jones have both scored four touchdowns.

If Notre Dame plans on having success against the Trojan defense, Eifert will have to be a big part of the game plan.

"(Against Wake Forest), we tried to get him the football, (and he) made incredible plays down the field," Kelly said of Eifert, who skipped a shot at the NFL draft after last season to return to Notre Dame. "(He's) a combination of a guy that understands Notre Dame, understands the value of a great education, and wanted to be on a championship football team. I think he epitomizes in terms of what we look for as a Notre Dame football player."

And he's a well-rounded, full-package tight end, to boot.

"What we find so often in tight ends is they're one or the other: They're big guys, really good blockers, or they're undersized guys that can run and catch a football," said Wake Forest coach Jim Grobe. "(Eifert's) the perfect combination. He's a good blocker. He did some good stuff in the run game, very athletic, and has some great hands. A great player, and one of the few tight ends that I've seen that has the ability he's got to not only block but catch the football."

The humility in Eifert forces him to deflect the praise.

"To (be a great tight end), you have to be able to block; catch the ball," Eifert said. "I'm still not there. I still have a lot of work to do. I think I've made a great improvement."

With the record out of the way, he can just relax and focus on his game.

The only numbers he needs to count now are the wins. ■

Tyler Eifert goes airborne to grab a first-quarter touchdown pass from Tommy Rees against BYU on Oct. 20. The score gave Notre Dame an early 7-0 lead. South Bend Tribune/JAMES BROSHER

NOVEMBER 17, 2012 • SOUTH BEND, INDIANA

NOTRE DAME 38, WAKE FOREST 0

Emotion And Domination

ND ascends to No. 1 after big win

By Eric Hansen

The senior victory lap was as disheveled as it was subdued, lost in the sea of yellow leis in the Notre Dame student section and a marshmallow fight in the stands that never seemed to end.

And it wasn't an accident. Sentimentality took a back seat to pragmatism, not that there weren't puddles of emotion left behind in third-ranked Notre Dame's most dominant, if not complete, victory of the season.

"The feeling is definitely different this year," Irish fifth-year senior wide receiver John Goodman said following a 38-0 Senior Day waxing of Wake Forest Saturday at Notre Dame Stadium. "We realize we have a lot to play for and a lot left in this season."

The stakes grew exponentially in the hours following the game.

First, unranked Baylor defrocked BCS No. 1 Kansas State, 52-24, in Waco, Texas. Then Stanford took down BCS No. 2 Or-

egon, 17-14, in overtime, putting the Irish (11-0) within a victory of playing for the national championship Jan. 7 in Miami and breaking down the door for them to jump all the way to No. 1 for the first time since falling to Boston College, 41-39, almost 19 years to the day.

Not that the Irish held anything back against the Demon Deacons (5-6), now losers of 32 successive games to top-five teams.

The Irish defense, the soul of ND's ascent from a preseason unranked team to one on the cusp of reaching the BCS National Championship Game likely against the SEC champ, reached a new benchmark Saturday. They held Wake to 209 total yards, the fewest allowed this season.

Wake's longest play was a 16-yard pass from quarterback Tanner Price to Michael Campanaro, the nation's seventh-leading receiver. The Deacons punted 10 times.

Linebacker Manti Te'o shows his appreciation to the Notre Dame Stadium fans as he takes a curtain call late in the game. The Heisman Trophy finalist said his desire to experience Senior Day was a significant factor in his decision to return to Notre Dame for his senior year. South Bend Tribune/JAMES BROSHER

And by pitching a shutout, the ND defense distinguished itself as having allowed the fewest points 11 games into a season—matched by the 1980 Irish—since coach Ara Parseghian's last national championship squad (1973) yielded 89.

All of which funnels into Notre Dame controlling its own destiny in its regular-season finale next Saturday against USC, a team whose chemistry has gone rancid after starting the season as the nation's No. 1 team in the AP poll.

The Trojans fell to 7-4 overall and out of contention for the Pac-12 championship game Saturday with a 38-28 loss to UCLA in which Trojans quarterback Matt Barkley suffered what *Los Angeles Daily News* reporter Scott Wolf is reporting as a separated right (throwing) shoulder.

"It's a game where we can actually do something and take this program to a place it hasn't been in a long time," said Irish senior linebacker Manti Te'o, ND's unorthodox Heisman Trophy candidate, who had six tackles before turning the defense over to the Irish reserves.

"We understand it's going to come down to the little things, really getting better every day."

The chronically fledgling Notre Dame offense did more than that. They arrived, conquered and flexed all in one game in missing a season-high in total yards (584) by three. And the missing piece, the one Kelly refused to give up on, continued to surge—sophomore quarterback Everett Golson.

In winning his ninth start in nine tries, he joins Kevin McDougal and Frank Tripucka and trails only Bob Williams (11) for the most consecutive wins as a starting Irish QB to start a career. More impressive, though, is his suddenly almost vertical growth curve.

Golson finished 20-of-30 for a career-high 346 passing yards and three touchdowns with one interception. Junior Tommy Rees came in in relief on a non-save situation with 7:14 left in the third quarter, followed by junior Andrew Hendrix and walk-on Charlie Fiessinger.

Golson's 317 first-half passing yards were 23 short of Jimmy Clausen's record for passing yards in a half set in 2009.

Irish tight end Tyler Eifert is dragged out of bounds by Demon Deacons defender Justin Jackson. Eifert caught six passes and moved past Ken MacAfee into first place on the school's career reception list for tight ends. South Bend Tribune/JAMES BROSHER

"We knew that he was going to be a problem for us with his feet, either running the ball or making plays outside the pocket," Wake Forest coach Jim Grobe offered. "I couldn't be more impressed with how accurately he threw the football, especially two or three deep balls.

"A couple of times, we thought we had a chance to get off the field, and he threw a couple of out routes that were money. They had some pretty good guys to throw it to."

Among them was senior tight end Tyler Eifert, who caught six passes and moved past former Irish All-American Ken MacAfee into first place on the school's career reception list for tight ends.

Senior Cierre Wood, who is eligible for a fifth year but hasn't indicated whether he'll exercise that option, collected 150 yards on 11 carries and leapfrogged Randy Kinder, George Gipp and Phil Carter Saturday into seventh place on the Irish career rushing list.

"I told them tonight I'm proud of them," said Kelly, whose team completed its first unbeaten run at Notre Dame Stadium since 1998. "I voted them No. 1 in the country for a reason, because I think they're the best team in the country, and I think they played like that tonight."

And they played at that level from the opening kick-off, before the tears had dried from the pregame embraces between the seniors and their parents.

Wood ripped off a 68-yard run on the fourth play of the game—the longest rush of the season by an Irish player—for a 7-0 Irish lead just 105 seconds into the game. Golson followed with touchdown passes to Eifert (two yards) and Goodman (50 yards) before the quarter was over. For the oft-injured Goodman, it was just his sixth reception of the season, half of which have gone for touchdowns.

The Irish rolled into halftime with a 31-0 advantage on the scoreboard and 430-113 in total yards.

"Everett played the best game of his life," Goodman said, "and it shows how much he's grown as a person and as a player. That just goes to show that he is taking his coaching and taking his leadership. He's that guy that we want to take us to the promised land." ■

Irish players have fun before singing the Alma Mater following Notre Dame's 38-0 win over Wake Forest in Notre Dame's final home game of 2012. South Bend Tribune/ROBERT FRANKLIN

HEAD COACH

BRIAN KELLY

Coach, Irish players acing remedial chemistry

By Eric Hansen • November 23, 2012

It was more of a slow cook than a microwaved moment, more of an evolution than a turning point. Undeniably, though, a Notre Dame football team that ended last season disjointed and started this one unranked stumbled upon its most elusive missing piece, then honed it, cherished it, built upon it and rode it all the way to the most profound moment in the program's timeline in the past 19 seasons.

And to think, an unrelenting team chemistry that camouflaged Notre Dame's flaws of inexperience while they incubated and has the top-ranked Irish (11-0) a win away from a berth in the BCS National Championship Game, Jan. 7 in Miami, started with loud voices and left an unsightly skidmark on social media 13 months ago.

The almost poetic symmetry is that both the nadir and genesis of the journey unfolded in the days following ND's 31-17 loss to USC last Oct. 22 in South Bend, a game that galvanized a late-season run by the Trojans, fueled a recruiting windfall and landed ND's archrivals as the AP poll's preseason No. 1 team for 2012.

Saturday night in the Los Angeles Memorial Coliseum, the two programs clash again, for the 84th time, with the script flipped.

The Irish are two games away from becoming the first FBS squad since BYU in 1984 to go from preseason unranked to national champs.

USC (7-4), unranked heading into its eighth encounter ever with a top-ranked ND squad (with a record of 2-5 in those games), is trying to avoid becoming the first preseason No. 1 team since Ole Miss in 1964 to finish on the outside of the rankings, looking in.

"That game in particular was certainly one where it required all of our players to really examine how they're going to be consistent winners," ND coach Brian Kelly said of last year's ND-USC matchup.

"I think they have obviously done an incredible job since that game. I don't know how many games we've lost since then, but it's not many. It was a great learning experience for everybody, including myself."

But not necessarily without pain.

Kelly's motivation for awkwardly drawing lines,

Irish head coach Brian Kelly communicates with quarterback Everett Golson during Notre Dame's April 21, 2012 Blue-Gold Game. Much of Notre Dame's success in 2012 can be traced to Kelly's more hands-on approach with his players. South Bend Tribune/ROBERT FRANKLIN

both with the media in an 8½-minute rant and behind closed doors with his team earlier that week, was to reinforce his long-term vision with his players and what it needed to look like to get there.

The unintended consequence was sequestering players into "Weis guys," recruited by former Irish coach Charlie Weis, and "Kelly guys."

The crack in team unity became a chasm as the conversation spilled onto Twitter. And that cyber-squawking included one of the faces of the eventual turnabout, one of the unifying voices in the months that ensued—Irish middle linebacker Manti Te'o.

"Playin for my bros and that's it!!!! @dflem45 @RobJob293 @Carlo44Cal @KLM_89 @Freekey_Zekey17 @stadium20status @J_Slaughter26 #the-originals" Te'o tweeted.

More players eventually joined in, with stronger, more pointed comments. A handful of former Irish players stoked the outrage.

Eventually, Kelly called a team meeting the Friday before a rout of Navy, reframed his comments and let the emotions from the players flow.

"I think that's when this team started to turn around, last year was when they had all the controversy about the team being split," said Irish center Braxston Cave. "A lot of guys had a lot of different opinions.

"But at the end of the day, everybody's here for the same reason. We all came together, and it was basically a conversation that if we all aren't together, then we're not going to get anywhere. From that day forward, the links reconnected."

And they've been tempered by events that were both designed to bring the team together and unexpected tests that tugged at the permanency of those bonds.

Among the latter was defensive end prodigy Aaron Lynch abruptly walking away from the program last April, roughly a week before the Notre Dame spring game, and eventually transferring to South Florida.

There were 11th-hour recruiting defections in January and February, the casting off of freshman cornerback Tee Shepard last March and sophomore offensive tackle Jordan Prestwood in August, long-term injuries to key players such as safeties Austin Collinsworth and Jamoris Slaughter, cornerback Lo Wood, tight end Alex Welch, defensive end Chase Hounshell, offensive tackle Tate Nichols and running back/USC transfer Amir Carlisle—all of whom figured, at the very least, to be in the Irish two-deeps.

There was a four-man quarterback derby, another potentially divisive exercise, followed by incumbent QB Tommy Rees' arrest, suspension and ultimate demotion to No. 2 on the depth chart.

"We knew we had a chance to do something special this year," Te'o said. "We weren't going to let anything get in our way."

But it's not that easy, at least not from a coaching standpoint.

Former Irish coach and current ESPN analyst Lou Holtz, whom Kelly called a valuable mentor earlier in the week, marveled at the way this ND team plays greater than the sum of its parts, but he remembers how much work goes in to creating those bonds.

"How often did I have to remind my teams about team chemistry?" Holtz pondered via telephone from his home in Orlando. "It may be best answered by, 'Was there ever a day I didn't have to remind them?' That's a constant battle. If I could go three hours without doing it, it's progress.

"The main thing is you don't have to like one another. You don't have to like the same music or the same food. But we have to share two things in common—one, the same goals and the second, our core values. The core values we had were: We're

"At Notre Dame, you have to be hands-on. There's no other way." —Lou Holtz

going to trust each other, we're going to be committed to excellence in everything we do, and we're going to care about each other."

And yet sometimes that's still not enough. The last time the Irish brought a No. 1 team into the L.A. Coliseum was 1988, with the Irish set to play an undefeated and No. 2-ranked USC team.

"One of my most vivid memories was that we flew commercial," Holtz said with a chuckle. "I also vividly remember sending two players home."

Those were stars Tony Brooks and Ricky Watters, who were late to a team meeting on Thanksgiving, before the team left for L.A., and then again for another team function on Friday night after the team had arrived in California.

"I didn't want to do it," Holtz said, "but if you give somebody your word—'if this happens one more time, you're going home'—you have no other choice but to honor your word. Because they broke their word, please don't ask me to break mine."

The Irish, without their fallen stars, defeated the Trojans 27-10.

Like Holtz, Kelly, from day one, set his sights on building a program long-term, not building toward a special season, then go receding back to the college football equivalent of the Thanksgiving kids' table. Like Auburn, for example—the 2010 national champs who bottomed out in the SEC this season.

It's been about awakening one of the sports' sleeping giants, a phase Oklahoma, Texas and Alabama have all experienced in the past decade or so.

If he had to do it all over again, Kelly would probably choose different words but not a different path. The hard line had to be drawn in the first two years, but just as necessary was Kelly's offseason introspection that ultimately provided the most essential piece to the chemistry experiment.

"I just think it started back in January, when I was committed to being a better head coach in the sense that I needed to spend more time with my players," he said just before camp started in August. "This job has a tendency to distract you a little bit, but I took it, because I wanted to coach and I wanted to be around the guys.

"Getting to know them better and letting them get to know me better, (rather) than just sitting up in the office and, 'Well, there's where the head coach at Notre Dame sits.' I've never been that kind of coach, and I felt myself sliding toward that in my first couple of years."

Holtz admitted he felt that happening toward the end of this time at ND, the result of being pulled in too many directions.

"At Notre Dame, you have to be hands-on," he said. "There's no other way."

There were other chemistry-builders for this Irish team—grueling workouts last summer in Notre Dame Stadium, goals and values posted on giant banners around the Guglielmino Athletics Complex. But the undersold story has been Kelly, reaching back to his past to reshape the future.

"I just need to be involved.… I need to be in the trenches," he said. "Some are better sitting up in the tower and some are better being hands-on. I need to be a better head coach, and that's what my strengths are. So I'm going to them." ■

NOVEMBER 24, 2012 · LOS ANGELES, CALIFORNIA

NOTRE DAME 22, USC 13

Irish Again Make A Stand

Defense sends ND to title matchup

By Bob Wieneke

Manti Te'o urged the Notre Dame fans to cheer louder. Brian Kelly distributed hugs. The Irish players sprinted toward their cheering section, one that serenaded the team with a loud "Let's Go Irish" as the clock wound down.

A surreal regular season ended with a reality that still feels like a dream. Top-ranked and 12-0 Notre Dame will play for the national championship, its 22-13 victory over USC Saturday night in front of a sellout crowd of 93,607 at the Los Angeles Memorial Coliseum clinching the trip to Miami for the Jan. 7 BCS Championship.

Yes, it was a joyous celebration on the field. And there was one in the locker room to match.

"It was," Irish coach Brian Kelly said, "as you would have expected."

Many didn't expect much out of this season. There was a tough schedule. There

were key losses to graduation and to injury. And the Irish were coming off back-to-back 8-5 seasons. Throw in uncertainty at quarterback.

Saturday night's victory over unranked and now 7-5 USC wasn't drop-dead gorgeous, but it certainly was beautiful in the eyes of the Irish.

The difference in this one? There were many.

It started and ended with ND's championship-caliber defense, which is one win away from simply being a championship defense. There were some penalties, but the exclamation point came late in the fourth quarter with the Trojans knocking on the door and trying to pull within 22-20.

The nation's stingiest defense — it entered the game allowing 10 points per game — kept the Trojans out of the end zone. Four plays from the Irish 1-yard line, including

Irish running back Theo Riddick finds a hole during Notre Dame's win over USC. The senior rushed for 146 yards on 20 carries. South Bend Tribune/JAMES BROSHER

Irish players celebrate with the Irish fan section following Notre Dame's 22-13 win over USC to complete a perfect 12-0 regular season. South Bend Tribune/JAMES BROSHER

three runs, were turned back. ND took over on downs with 2:33 left.

"Unbelievable goal-line stand," Kelly said.

Special teams made a significant contribution. Kyle Brindza kicked five field goals, including a 52-yarder on the final play of the first half that is the second-longest in school history. His five field goals tied a school record, making it the fifth time an Irish kicker has kicked that many field goals in a game.

He now has 23 on the season, two more than John Carney's single-season school record.

Then there was the quarterback play. Last year, when USC won in South Bend, Matt Barkley was considered the difference. This year, both teams started redshirt freshmen, but ND's Everett Golson was making his 10th career start, SC's Max Wittek his first.

Wittek threw two interceptions, while Golson, who wasn't as statistically dazzling as he was last week against Wake Forest, remained unbeaten (10-0) as a starter. Only Bob Williams has won more consecutive starts as an Irish QB (11) to start a career.

If you're handing out helmet stickers, though, start with senior running back Theo Riddick. Heck, give him two. Riddick who gained tough yards early and just kept on gaining tough yards throughout as Notre Dame built an early lead and never relinquished it. Riddick finished with 146 rushing yards on 20 carries and 33 more on three receptions.

Riddick's nine-yard touchdown run late in the first quarter put the Irish up 10-0.

After USC scored on the first play of the second quarter to trim ND's lead to 10-7, it was a battle to maintain the lead, a battle the Irish won, which in turn won them a trip to Miami.

Unranked at the beginning of the season, ND charged up the polls, reaching No. 1 last week after Oregon and Kansas State, the two teams ahead of it in the BCS standings, lost on the same night.

That put destiny in the hands of the Irish, and they didn't let go.

"Ecstatic," Riddick said outside the Irish locker room. "That's the only word I can say right now." ■

With only the USC Trojans standing between the Irish and a berth in the BCS National Championship Game, Notre Dame players wait to take the field at the Los Angeles Memorial Coliseum. South Bend Tribune/JAMES BROSHER

Finishing Second In Heisman Didn't Mute Te'o's Message Or Legacy

By Eric Hansen • December 9, 2012

On a night that could have been the pinnacle in a career that has taken a dizzying, almost vertical, ascent, Manti Te'o almost made history twice.

Hours before Texas A&M 20-year-old redshirt freshman quarterback Johnny Manziel denied the Notre Dame senior linebacker the distinction of being the first exclusively defensive player ever to win the Heisman Trophy, Saturday night at the Best Buy Theater, the event organizers politely but firmly denied the Laie, Hawaii, native his desire to dress for success in the manner in which he wanted.

Wearing an i'e.

That's a toga-like mat popular in Samoan culture, or as Te'o himself called it "a skirt thing worn by the men" on special occasions. Occasions that include weddings, funerals, building of new houses, church events, tattooing, and appointing of a new chief in a village.

But apparently not Heisman coronations.

"They asked me to just wear this," he said of his tux, which he subsequently adorned with a yellow lei and a green garland draped over his shoulders that was so massive it looked like it was wrested from Wrigley Field. "They just didn't think it would be appropriate for this event."

It turned out to be Manziel's night anyway, at least where the 928-person Heisman electorate was concerned. Manziel, only the third freshman to be invited to New York as a finalist since that practice started in 1982, walked away as the first freshman to actually win the award.

Manziel amassed 2,029 points and 474 first-place votes, winning all but one of the six geographical regions—the Midwest. He was named first, second or third on 92 percent of the ballots.

"I came a long way," Te'o said afterward. "That's something to look at. Congratulations to Johnny. He deserves it. He had a wonderful season, and I'm just relieved. Now it's time to get ready for 'Bama.

"I can't really describe it. It's that burn that's saying 'You've got to get better.' It's motivation. I always wanted to be the best, and I'll use it as motivation to be the best I can be. I have a lot of work to do and I'm just excited to get back and get things cracking."

The top-ranked Irish (12-0) face No. 2 but 10-point favorite Alabama (12-1) Jan. 7 in the BCS National Championship Game at Miami.

Instead of Te'o becoming the eighth Heisman winner for Notre Dame, he settles in as the fourth runner-up in school history and the first since wide

Manti Te'o addresses the crowd at Purcell Pavilion during the pep rally before Notre Dame's final home game against Wake Forest. South Bend Tribune/JAMES BROSHER

Manti Teo's impact on Notre Dame stretched beyond the gridiron. A popular figure on campus, he was also active in the South Bend community. On Nov. 29, Te'o and teammate Louis Nix III, playing the part of Santa Claus, posed for a photo during the Silent Night Silent Auction, an annual fundraiser held by Notre Dame's Pasquerilla East dormitory benefiting the American Cancer Society's Relay for Life. South Bend Tribune/JAMES BROSHER

receiver/kick returner Rocket Ismail got nosed out for the 1990 award by BYU quarterback Ty Detmer, a month before Te'o came bounding into this life.

The other two ND second-place finishers were Angelo Bertelli (1941), two years before he was named the winner, and Joe Theismann (1970).

Te'o was named on 84 percent of the ballots and garnered 1,706 points, the third-most ever by a runner-up and the most ever by a purely defensive player. His 321 first-place votes were the second-most accumulated by a second-place finisher in the award's 78-year history.

Kansas State senior quarterback Collin Klein was third with 894 points (60 first-place votes),

followed by USC wide receiver Marqise Lee (207) and Ohio State quarterback Braxton Miller (144), both sophomores.

Preseason favorite, USC quarterback Matt Barkley, didn't finish in the top 10, nor did early-season runaway leader, West Virginia quarterback Geno Smith. Two defensive players besides Te'o did— South Carolina defensive end Jadeveon Clowney (sixth) and Georgia linebacker Jarvis Jones (10th).

"This is a moment I've dreamed about since I was a little kid in the back yard pretending to be Doug Flutie and throwing Hail Marys to my dad," Manziel said in the moments after he made history.

Manziel and his family also continually tipped

their caps to Te'o, who befriended the Aggies QB and invited him to go cliff jumping in Oahu sometime in the offseason, a development that might scare Texas A&M coach Kevin Sumlin more than letting Manziel be quoted.

Up until a couple of weeks ago, Sumlin wouldn't let Manziel or any of his other freshmen do media interviews.

Manziel's father, meanwhile, wore a string of Kukui nuts around his neck, while his mother donned a lei, both beloved symbols in Te'o's broadening world.

And once the sting fades, the lasting memory of Te'o's improbable Heisman run connects back to home—both his South Bend one and the people back on the North Shore of Oahu.

"That's what I want to do, affect people," Te'o said. "I don't care about the tackles. I don't care about the interceptions. All I care is the impact I have on lives, especially the people back home."

Sometimes he does more than merely impact them. Sometimes he changes a life's trajectory.

There was the little girl at the South Bend Center for the Homeless in June of 2010 that he let climb on him like a jungle gym as they watched the movie "Finding Nemo" together on a rainy day.

"I want to be a TV star," she told him, showing off a smile that seemed to sparkle, even with two front teeth missing. "What do you think?"

Te'o told her that day to dream big. On Saturday night, he showed just what can happen if you do.

Then there's Micaela Kauhane, a fourth-grader at Punahou School when Te'o was a senior there. He was her mentor that year in a school-sponsored program, and Te'o promised her that he would give her his playing gloves after Punahou won the state title.

Not only did Te'o remember and keep the promise in the emotional moments following what was then the biggest victory of his life, he stayed in touch with Micaela and her best friend, Rachel, long after the program ended.

"When I go home, I usually take her and Rachel out to McDonald's," Te'o said. "They always want to go to McDonald's. I take them to McDonald's and get a bite to eat and just make sure they don't got boyfriends.

"I'm like their big brother, and she's just a beautiful soul. When you see kids, there's an innocence about them that's just amazing. It reminds you how life used to be and how life was great and you didn't have all of this on your shoulders."

Micaela didn't forget the kindness. Now an eighth-grader and burgeoning long-distance runner, she and Rachel surprised Te'o by flying to Los Angeles with family and cheering him on in ND's 22-13 victory at USC, the win that sealed the national title game berth.

Back home in Laie Saturday, in the Te'o family's yard to be exact, family and friends stood 30 deep in anticipation of another defiant burst at conventional thinking by Te'o and Notre Dame in a season full of them. Elsewhere around Oahu, T-shirts celebrating Te'o's stab at history, both of the legal and unlicensed variety, were popping up seemingly at every corner.

"His impact is above and beyond anything we've ever seen, at least within the era in which I've been covering sports," said Honolulu TV reporter Steve Uyehara, whose TV station, Hawaii News Now, made the 11-hour flight to cover Te'o.

"On the way here, (fellow reporter) Mike Cherry and I were walking through the airport in Honolulu. And a bunch of flight attendants saw us and they saw our cameras, and they knew exactly what we were doing. They started chanting, 'Manti, Manti, Manti.'

"He's a rock star there. Whatever he does, he wants to make an impact. He's using his stage to do that. Whatever he says, people will listen."

And when they listen, they tend to believe.

On Friday and Saturday, Te'o's path crossed with four of ND's former Heisman Trophy winners—John Lattner, Paul Hornung, John Huarte and Tim Brown.

Perhaps strangely, the Heisman Trophy never came up in conversation. Instead they thanked Te'o for his team sticking together. They thanked him and the team for overcoming adversity. And they thanked him for bringing Notre Dame football back—in their minds—for good. ■

JANUARY 7, 2013 • MIAMI GARDENS, FLORIDA

BCS NATIONAL CHAMPIONSHIP GAME • ALABAMA 42, NOTRE DAME 14

ND Season Ends in Heartbreak

Irish shortcomings exposed in epic BCS blowout

By Eric Hansen

They could have been forever's team, larger than life and sculpted to look like those black-and-white pictures in a scrapbook.

And maybe they still will be remembered like that — someday.

So thorough, though, was top-ranked Notre Dame's plummet Monday night off the grandest stage that Irish football had climbed onto in almost a quarter of a century, the stench of the impending social media snark, the punch lines, the bewilderment will be hard to shake for a while.

The most painful and most shocking facet of No. 2 Alabama's 42-14 romp to dynasty status was that it made the very heart of ND's ascendance from unranked to top-ranked — its defensive front seven — look like a mirage.

And in the anticlimactic aftermath, the question that chased the Irish almost all the way along their journey to Miami, returned and reverberated through cyberspace as Monday night spilled into Tuesday morning.

Is Notre Dame football really back?

"Definitely, we're close," said Irish All-America linebacker Manti Te'o, the face and the soul of ND's renaissance. "Obviously, we're not there. Otherwise if we were there, we would be holding the crystal (trophy).

"But if we weren't close, we definitely wouldn't be in South Beach. And I know coach (Brian) Kelly and Everett (Golson) and all of the guys who are coming back, they're just going to be that much better and it's going to be exciting to watch them next year."

A record Sun Life Stadium crowd of 80,120, that pulsated pregame in anticipation of the clash of cultures and traditions in the second-to-last ever BCS National Championship Game, was reduced to a collection

Alabama running back Eddie Lacy tries to break away from Notre Dame defensive backs KeiVarae Russell, left, and Zeke Motta during the first half. Lacy was the game's leading rusher, totaling 140 yards on 20 attempts. South Bend Tribune/JAMES BROSHER

Fighting Irish quarterback Everett Golson tries to escape the grasp of Alabama's C.J. Mosley. Golson faced pressure from the Crimson Tide defensive front all night. South Bend Tribune/JAMES BROSHER

of golf clappers as Alabama (13-1) gashed the nation's No. 1 scoring defense — early, often and convincingly — on the way to its third national title in four years and 15th overall by its own count.

Four seconds into the second quarter, the Irish (12-1) had been outscored 21-0, outgained 202-23, had a 10-1 deficit in first downs and trailed in time of possession 12:08 to 2:52. All this against an ND team that held a collective 85-9 edge in the first quarter for the season, coming in.

Suddenly, a game that commanded such intrigue that Daniel "Rudy" Ruettiger couldn't score a ticket (per *The New Yorker*), turned into a Bob Davie-esque flashback. When the Alabama lead reached 35-0 at the 5:37 mark of the third quarter, it represented the largest point differential at any point in any of the 15 BCS National Championship Games.

The Irish, who hadn't yielded so much as 400 total yards in a game, were squeezed for 529. They were out-rushed 265-32, making Alabama coach Nick Saban 50-0 since the start of the 2008 season when his teams reach the 150-yard mark in rushing and 11-7 otherwise.

The Tide blew past the 150-yard mark early in the third quarter. Both Eddie Lacy, named the game's most outstanding offensive player, and sidekick T.J. Yeldon broke the 100-yard plateau. Alabama' vaunted offensive line was better than advertised — way better.

"That was probably the biggest surprise to me, how we were able to control the line of scrimmage," said Alabama coach Nick Saban. "I think their guys got a little tired earlier in the game. I think it might be easier for us to play in those conditions — the humidity — because that's what we grow up with."

What Kelly characterized as a serious knee injury knocked Irish defensive end Kapron Lewis-Moore out of the game in the second quarter and perhaps out of the NFL Draft. But by then, the Tide wasn't just rolling, it was steamrolling.

Irish running back Theo Riddick takes to the air to gain yardage in the first half. The senior was limited to 37 rushing yards on 10 carries. South Bend Tribune/JAMES BROSHER

Crimson Tide receiver Christion Jones beats Notre Dame defender Elijah Shumate to haul in a catch during the first half. Alabama quarterback AJ McCarron completed 20 of 28 passes. South Bend Tribune/JAMES BROSHER

THE SEASON THAT BROUGHT NOTRE DAME BACK

The counterpunchless Irish start fed into the SEC superiority complex for both the Crimson Tide and its fan base, many of whom looked at Notre Dame as little more than Mississippi State with shinier helmets coming into the game.

The statistical carnage was in line with ND's three previous BCS meltdowns. In ND's four BCS losses — all by 14 points or more and three of them by at least 27 points — the Irish have been outgained 2198-1178 and outrushed 941-326.

If there were threads of hope, they were surprisingly on the offensive side of the ball. Golson didn't wither and threw for 270 yards. He ran for one of the Irish TDs and threw for the other.

In DaVaris Daniels' first game back from a Nov. 10 broken collarbone, the sophomore collected six catches for 115 yards. Tight end Tyler Eifert, meanwhile, leaped over two Irish legends — Heisman Trophy winner Tim Brown and Jim Seymour — finishing his career in sixth place on ND's all-time receptions list.

But they were obscured by a puzzling big picture, one Kelly is convinced Notre Dame will learn from and build upon rather than repeat.

"It sets a bar for your entire program, because we all now know what we need to do to move from where we are," he said, "which is a 12-0 football team, a pretty good football team, but not good enough.

"So it's clear what we need to do in the offseason. It's clear what we need to do with player development. It's clear that we need to coach better and recruit. It's a great, great opportunity that we had here.

"It's disappointing that we lost the football game, but it's going to make my job very easy when it comes to talking to players about how you win a national championship." ■

Eddie Lacy breaks away from Irish safety Matthias Farley to score one of his two first-half touchdowns. South Bend Tribune/ JAMES BROSHER

Alabama's T.J. Yeldon dives into the end zone. The score gave Alabama a 21-0 second-quarter lead. South Bend Tribune/ROBERT FRANKLIN

BCS Game Gave Golson Chance to Grow

By Al Lesar

Growth can be a painful process.

Everett Golson's learning curve as the redshirt freshman quarterback with the Notre Dame football team had its peaks and valleys.

Where he begins the 2013 season will be critical to the Irish success.

With a running game that was shut down and held to just 32 net yards, Golson directed a Notre Dame offense against Alabama in the BCS National Championship Game with one arm figuratively tied behind his back.

Dealing with that situation, which resulted in a 42-14 loss, will be an experience the 6-foot, 185-pounder will be able to draw on down the road.

Golson accounted for most of the Irish offense, connecting on 21 of 36 passes for 270 yards and a touchdown. More than numbers, Golson came away from the game's biggest stage with plenty of experience.

"The experience, being here, playing the game, seeing where the bar is — I took a lot away from it," Golson said. "Next year, I'm stepping into that role of being a leader."

Without much to gain at halftime, Irish offensive coordinator Chuck Martin issued his quarterback a challenge.

"I pulled (Golson) aside at halftime, 'This is 30 more minutes of unbelievable practice against the national champion,'" Martin said. "We have no run game, we're down 28-0, they're mixing coverages. It's better than we could ever (simulate in practice).

"I thought he took huge advantage, made a bunch of plays and did a bunch of great things."

Golson is now able to file away those memories.

"If we really want what we say we want, we have to play teams like this," Golson said. "The bar is set and try to get over it. Not meet it, get over it."

"The future's bright based on how far we've come in a short time," said Martin. "If we got this far with an inexperienced guy, how far can we go when we get him (seasoned)?

"He did a lot of good things; managed the game. Keep everything going and don't take your foot off the gas.

"This fall camp we were teaching him everything. Next fall camp will have a different feel. He's going to come in and get a lot better. We're excited."

"It definitely adds (fuel to the fire)," Golson said. "To know that it's not me coming home with the crystal ball (national championship trophy), it's going to make me work harder in the offseason."

No substitute for hard work as development happens. ■

Irish quarterback Everett Golson pitches the ball during the first half of the BCS National Championship Game. The first-year quarterback completed 21 of 36 passes for 270 yards. South Bend Tribune/JAMES BROSHER

Notre Dame's George Atkinson III is taken down on a kick return. The sophomore — expected to take on a larger role in the Irish offense in 2013 — returned three kicks a total of 47 yards against the Crimson Tide. South Bend Tribune/JAMES BROSHER